THE SOCIAL MESSAGE OF
THE MODERN PULPIT

THE SOCIAL MESSAGE OF THE MODERN PULPIT

BY

CHARLES REYNOLDS BROWN

FIRST CONGREGATIONAL CHURCH
OAKLAND, CALIFORNIA

CHARLES SCRIBNER'S SONS
NEW YORK 1911

TO

Alice Tufts Brown

PREFACE

WHEN the invitation to deliver the Lyman Beecher Lectures at Yale University for the year 1905–6 came to me, I very naturally, in the selection of a theme, consulted the main lines of interest in my own work as a Christian minister. I have been for some years especially interested in expository preaching as a suitable and profitable method of presenting religious truth to a congregation, and in the application of the principles of the Gospel to social conditions. After consultation with the Dean of the Faculty, it seemed to me possible to combine both of these interests in the course of lectures which I was asked to give.

I have accordingly embodied in this course a brief study of the Book of Exodus, dealing with it entirely on the sociological side, both as an illustration of this method of relating ancient Scripture to modern life and for the sake of the real content of the book as it bears upon " the social message of the modern pulpit," which is my main theme.

I am deeply indebted to many older and wiser men who have studied and worked in the field of interest here traversed, a number of whom I have quoted in this volume. I also wish to express my personal gratitude to two laymen in my own congregation—Mr. Charles Z. Merritt and Mr. Warren Olney, Jr.—who were so kind as to read the lectures before they were delivered, and to give me the benefit of many helpful criticisms and valuable suggestions.

In the course of the discussion I have naturally touched upon many controverted points. It is needless to say that no responsibility whatever for the opinions expressed attaches to the members of the faculty of the Yale Divinity School, although nothing could have exceeded their kindness and courtesy to me in connection with the service which I had been asked to render.

It is my own conviction that the Christian minister in these days occupies a position where rare privilege and serious responsibility are mingled in an unusual way—the average pastor is neither a capitalist nor a wage earner, neither an employer nor an employé, as those terms are currently used; and he is therefore in a position where he ought to be able to render a genuine service to all those parties in interest whose personal fortunes are more directly involved in the problems here discussed than are his

own. If in any slight degree I have in these lectures
made plainer this opportunity for usefulness, or
brought out more clearly the obligation resting upon
all who have it in their power to aid in any wise in
the solution of these problems, one of the important
ends aimed at in the course will have been secured.

In sending the lectures out in book form, I do it
in the hope that, while they were originally given
in a divinity school, they may come into the hands
of many laymen interested, as they are at present,
in all these social questions.

CHARLES REYNOLDS BROWN.

CONTENTS

THE SOCIAL MESSAGE OF THE MODERN PULPIT

CHAPTER I

THE NEED OF MORAL LEADERSHIP IN SOCIAL EFFORT

IN almost every period of the world's life there are certain movements of thought and feeling which may be called glacial. They are widespread; they cannot be successfully resisted; they leave their mark upon the face of the whole region they traverse. The teachers of religion at such a time will not gain their highest effectiveness by acting in utter independence of such movements—in so far as these movements embody wholesome elements and are in any wise headed toward the main goal, the true prophets of the period will act with them. If religion is to make itself widely and profoundly useful, it must ally itself openly and intelligently with those common, fundamental interests which God in His Providence or the Holy Spirit in His supreme guidance, has brought to the fore.

1

The time-spirit and the Holy Spirit are not as a rule identical, but they are not necessarily antagonistic, nor are they likely to be altogether independent. When we take into consideration the deeper and more permanent elements in the time-spirit, we shall more commonly find its relation to the Holy Spirit to be one which is subordinate but harmonious. The true prophet, therefore, will actively seek the guidance of that Spirit of Truth which is everlasting, and he will also study the signs of the times—study them, it is to be hoped, with more discernment than was manifested by those superficial observers referred to in the Scriptures who were only enabled by their outlook upon " the signs of the times " to make a shrewd guess as to to-morrow's weather. The prophet's genuine knowledge of his own time will serve to make his utterances pertinent and practical, while his abiding fellowship with that Spirit of Truth, which is from everlasting to everlasting, will give them enduring strength and vitality.

Now the social interest which occupies so large a part of the world's mind to-day, and the social sympathy which has such a profound hold upon its heart, and the social energy which absorbs so much of the strength of its right arm, constitute, in my judgment, just such a movement for the times on which we have fallen.   Thirty years ago physical science was to the fore in the popular interest. The Athenians of that day spent the major part of their time either in telling or in hearing "some new thing" in geology or biology or astronomy. The pulpits of that day were unnecessarily and unprofitably busy in adjusting matters between Moses and Darwin, or in bringing about labored "reconciliations" between science and religion. Happily all this is now changed. The work of physical science is still carried forward, but the dominant interest to-day is fixed upon the organized life of men. The mood of the hour is one of fraternal sympathy, and it behooves the prophets of religion not only to harness these warm, strong, widely diffused feelings to useful lines of effort, but to discover their deeper relations and to ally them with the spiritual aspiration of the race. A resolute public sentiment has taken up certain problems to which other generations have been to a great extent indifferent; it has set them out in bold relief to be seen, to be discussed, to be solved! And if religion is to be made deeply and widely effective in these days, it is imperative that this absorbing social interest should be recognized, utilized, and brought within the power of a noble consecration.

I esteem this duty so fundamental that I should not hesitate to say that the willingness and the ability of its ministers to serve as useful leaders in this

important service is the supreme need of the modern
church.   I am not unmindful of other needs.   It
is important that there should be some definite re-
statement of certain essential truths and a strong conviction regarding their saving influence.   It is important that in many communions there should be
some readjustment of polity, making room for the
ever-growing spirit of democracy within an organization sufficiently close knit for effective service.   It
is important that this luxury-loving age should be
brought up to a more generous consecration of its
means to the enlarging demands of that benevolent
work which the modern emphasis on philanthropic
effort has inaugurated.   It is important that there
should be kindled, or rekindled, a genuine passion
for souls which shall produce not a perfunctory
nor a hysterical but a true evangelism in all the
churches.   It is important that there should be a
deeper spiritual life pervading all the religious bodies,
cordially relating itself to the moods and the methods
of these modern times.   In all that I have to say
in this series of lectures, I do not for a moment ignore
or minimize any of these needs.   But I believe the
supreme need of the hour is for men who have the
wisdom, the courage, and the conscience requisite to
guide the Christian forces of the country in making
thorough application of the principles of the Gospel

terest. They held their possessions in trust for the common good, no man saying that anything was exclusively his own. They parted their possessions as every man had need, so that there was none among them that lacked.

It does not diminish the significance of this social movement in the early Christian Church to say that, unlike certain modern schemes, it was a voluntary communism; or that it was tried in a small community of high-minded people, all filled with the Spirit; or that they wrought with a simple rather than with an intricate industrial organization. It does not discredit it to say that it was undertaken in the expectation that the whole *régime* under which they were living would soon be terminated by the visible return of Christ, or to say that it does not seem to have been a financial success. All these comments and criticisms upon the undertaking I accept and believe. But however different the conditions of their life from our own, and whatever may have been their lack of economic wisdom, that brave attempt of theirs does make plain this fact, that people filled with the Holy Ghost regard it as imperative that they should at once strive to make their industrial relations, their ordinary use of their property, and their whole attitude toward the less capable members of society a direct expression of the will of God concerning them, and of the spirit of Jesus Christ now resident within their hearts. Both the Jewish and the Christian churches at the very outset thus esteemed the thorough application of the social principles in the divine message they had received a primary and a fundamental duty.

I believe we touch here what is the supreme need of the modern church if it is to be the highest agent of the divine will in the establishment of that kingdom which is to include and consecrate all these common interests. People to-day cannot run away from injustice and oppression as the ancient Israelites did —there is no Canaan for them to go to, since even the wide spaces of our own great West have been so completely appropriated by private ownership; they must have it out with Pharaoh right here. They cannot separate themselves into small communities after the fashion of the early Christians at Jerusalem, or of the Shakers or Ruskinites, in order to practise communism. This is simply impossible for the many; and those who do withdraw only leave the rest of us to fight the battle without their aid. We cannot, if we would, take the wings of the dove and fly away to be at rest, in any sort of peaceful retreat—we can only stay where we are and pray that the Spirit, which is like a dove, shall come upon us in the very thick of these domestic and social, these industrial and political problems, teaching us consideration for one another's interests, and guiding us in those courses of action which make for the realization of the kingdom of God on earth. And the readiness and fitness of the prophets of the faith to serve as moral leaders in this high undertaking I regard as one of the most important elements in their ministerial equipment.

This form of service is demanded by the churches in order to make religion widely effective among all classes of men, thus promoting a genuine revival of interest and of power in the land. Every great revival in the past has had some one dominant idea which in its essence embodied a strong demand for personal righteousness. In the Great Awakening under Jonathan Edwards it was divine sovereignty. God is King: " Thou shalt worship the Lord thy God, and him only shalt thou serve." In the revival under John Wesley it was human freedom. Men can vote in the great election: " Whosoever will may come." In the revival under Charles G. Finney it was personal responsibility. Men make or mar their own destinies: " The soul that sinneth it shall die, but he that doeth that which is lawful and right shall save his soul alive." In the revival under Dwight L. Moody it was the divine mercy. There is an infinite compassion for all our moral failure: " God so loved the world, that he gave his only begotten son, that whosoever believeth on him should not perish, but have everlasting life." In the next great revival which will quicken the country into new religious life, I believe the dominant note will be that of social responsibility, and the two main texts of the movement will be: " We are all members one of another," and " One is our Master, even Christ, and all we are brethren." That revival, when it comes, will, in my judgment, embody the strongest demand for personal righteousness the world has ever felt—it will lay hold upon that great word of Christ in Gethsemane, " For *their* sakes, I sanctify myself! "

It does not seem possible to-day to kindle the interest of the more thoughtful people to any considerable degree, or to make the church life really aggressive, or to arouse deeply the hearts of the ministers themselves, except as the religious efforts proposed have steadily in view something wider than individual peace and paradise. It is almost impossible to stir the individual outside the church or to stimulate the efforts of others on his behalf, so long as the issue is largely one of personal security, present or eternal. But once let that larger note come in which Jesus struck at the opening of his ministry, " Repent, for the kingdom of heaven is at hand "—

about face, because a better order awaits its realization through the efforts of renewed men; once let the modern herald begin to cry, ' The Spirit of the Lord is upon me because he hath anointed me to preach good tidings to the poor; he hath sent me to bind up the brokenhearted, to preach deliverance to the captives and to set at liberty them that are bruised, and to usher in the acceptable year of the Lord '; once let that larger note come in strongly and distinctly—and there is sure to be an immediate kindling of interest.

Ministers of religion are sent out to be fishers of men. But when they use exclusively those methods which lay the sole or even the main emphasis upon individual regeneration, leaving social problems to be worked out sometime, somewhere, quite apart from the inspiration and guidance of the Christian Church, I think you will bear me witness that in these days they do not land the fish to any considerable extent; and in certain classes of society they do not land them at all.

It is easy to lay the blame for this failure on others. It is easy to say that such methods have been owned and blessed of God; they worked once and would work now, were it not for the hard and un-circumcised hearts of these twentieth-century fish. It is easy to say that the age is altogether material in its aims; that it lacks high aspirations, and is ungodly in the extreme—it has always been easier to call men hard names than to win them to higher levels of experience. It is easy to denounce roundly the pleasure-seekers and the social agitators who, in their different ways, have done much to draw away the attention of thousands of people from the Christian Church—it is especially easy to do this from the pulpit, because the people denounced are not usually there to hear. But none of these excuses for the failure of the minister to gain a hearing for, and the acceptance of, his message ever satisfies the heart of a man who is hungry to win other men to Christ.

The trite criticism that while Peter converted three thousand men with one sermon it now takes, according to the painful figures in the denominational year-books, almost three thousand sermons to convert one man, is hurled at preachers who are already humiliated by their apparent lack of effectiveness. But where in all God's world has any minister in the last ten years ever preached to any congregation that had in it three thousand unconverted men? The great evangelists have all found that when they spoke in the largest halls and churches to be had, these places were for the main part filled up with professing Christians. And if the Christians had all stayed away, we feel no assurance that those who are not Christians would have occupied the seats.

Yet all the while there were gatherings in all the large cities, where three thousand men who were not professing Christians did come together for the consideration of problems which bear vitally on moral and spiritual life. Whenever I see or hear of such an assembly, I feel that as fishers of men we ought to be able to approach that stream of modern life, which runs bank-full and swift, with such tackle and such bait, with such sympathetic knowledge of those interests, and such ability to speak the language in which they were born, that we, too, could take those men in larger numbers, to the glory and honor of Christ. And the ability of the modern minister to do just that is a fundamental need if we are to make religion widely effective and thus promote a genuine revival which shall touch all classes of society.

This type of leadership, in the work of applying the social principles of the Gospel, is also demanded in view of the fact that the pathway to spiritual life for great masses of people is blocked for lack of just this. It was a sombre word which the author of the Book of Exodus uttered at one point in his story: " The Egyptians made the children of Israel to serve with rigor and they made their lives bitter with hard service. . . . And the Israelites hearkened not unto

Moses for anguish of spirit." The appeal of the prophet who came to guide them into the land of promise and into a higher life was for a time altogether unheeded because the people were in no condition to respond. The good seed fell by the wayside and the rigor of their industrial condition devoured it up. The utter physical exhaustion, the dull, sodden nature induced by years of cheerless toil, the lack of zest for any but the coarser gratifications of the flesh which brought the relaxation they craved, the want of outlook or prospect, all these made the task of producing spiritual values in that generation well nigh hopeless. As a matter of fact all the men of that generation, except two, died in the wilderness of doubt and disobedience—they "hearkened not unto Moses for anguish of spirit and for cruel bondage."

And all this is not by any means mere ancient history. It is a just characterization of whole sections of our modern workaday world. The city pastor finds it hard, oftentimes, to urge some workingman to become a Christian and to think upon high and holy themes when he sees the house the man lives in, the mill he works in, the streets his children play in, and the general atmosphere in which they all move. It seems to him as if something a shade stronger than John Calvin's "Irresistible

Grace " would be demanded to enable such a man to respond with eagerness to the call of the Spirit.

If you will take the trouble to go through the section of the city where the operatives in some factory are housed and see with your own eyes the actual conditions of their lives; if you will visit the homes where by pressure of want the mother is also thrust into the mill with several of her young children besides; if you will stand by as they take their pleasures and witness their poverty, not only in things material but in all the finer values of life, you will need no commentary to tell you the meaning of that statement in Exodus as to the unresponsiveness of certain hearts because of the conditions of their toil.   The spiritual tragedy which stands ugly and bare in whole sections of the worker's world is the most awful aspect of it. With these thousands of weary, beaten, and baffled men and women in mind, it seems like a cruel joke when we get together in our ministerial associations and read fancy little papers on " How to Reach the Masses," deciding, perhaps, that it can be done with a little more music, or a bit more of advertising, or with more hand-shaking at the door of the church. Thousands of them hearken not to the prophet " for anguish of spirit and for cruel bondage "! The application of Christian principles to social conditions is therefore demanded because their pathway to spiritual life is blocked for lack of it.

This type of leadership is also needed by the church, because that deeper spiritual life which it craves for itself can best be realized through such wisely directed social service. Spiritual life, I take it, is knowing and enjoying the presence of the Spirit of God within the heart. There may be many ways of gaining this experience—there are differences of administration for different individuals and for different eras—by the same Spirit. The dominant mood of this present time, referred to above, indicates, to my mind, that the most direct pathway to spirituality for the majority of Christians to-day lies through rightly ordered social service.

We would all agree, no doubt, that the three main manifestations which God has made of Himself thus far are these: He revealed Himself in the world about us—this is the work of God. He revealed Himself in literature, and we have in our Bible what is called distinctively " the word of God." He revealed Himself in a personal life, and we have in Jesus of Nazareth " the Son of God." To-day He is revealing Himself mainly in the associated life of men, so that there will come at last, as the fourth great manifestation, the " kingdom " or " the household of God." The work of god, the word of God, the Son of God, and the kingdom of God—through these we are to see the material, the literary, the personal, and the corporate expressions of the life of God in the world.

Now if the mind of the Spirit is in any wise reflected in the dominant interest of great numbers of clear-headed, pure-hearted people at the present time, we may believe that, while we are gratefully to accept and utilize all that God has shown us of Himself in His work and in His word and in His Son, we are, with the strength thus gained, to press forward to the fuller realization of His presence and power among us by our coöperation with Him for the establishment of His kingdom. We are to find and know Him, we are to love and serve Him, in the very gaining of that better order which is to stand as the fairest expression of His will the world has yet seen—men organized and acting together in the spirit of Christ! Such a consummation will be the realization of that great prayer in Gethsemane—that we should all be one, in the spirit of mutual consideration and helpfulness, even as He and the Father are One. It will be, in finite measure, the supreme manifestation of the entirety of God's life, for His Spirit and purpose will stand most fully revealed in those broad areas of a redeemed social life. And thus to serve wisely and faithfully the interests of that coming kingdom, aiding in its advance, is indeed to know the living God in a deeper spiritual life.

The prophet of old sounded this note. You will recall the word of Jeremiah: " He judged the cause of the poor and needy; then it was well with him. Was not this to know Me, saith the Lord? " Social effort is here defined and approved as the straight road into knowing God—knowing Him not by the intellectual mastery of His attributes but by sharing in His power and wisdom and love through useful service. Social effort ought always to be so outlined by the teachers of religion and so entered upon by the followers of Christ that it will be no more a gross fight for material advantage, nor a mere temporary relief of pressing want. It ought rather to be the religion of One who said, " Inasmuch as ye did it unto one of the least of these," rising into larger reality in the every-day life of the world. ' Judge the cause of the poor and the needy,' the Spirit is saying unto the churches, ' then it shall be well with thee for thus ye shall come to know me.' In doing just that in the spirit of Christ, the people in the churches will know more perfectly that Lord whose tender interest is over and within all those who need this humane service.

I shall always remember a serious talk with an intelligent Christian layman in an Eastern city. His father and his grandfather had been Congregational ministers, and he was himself an active member of one of our churches there. He enjoyed regularly and gratefully the ministrations of one of the most spiritually minded pastors in that city. He was telling me of the Christian work in which he had been engaged the winter before. He had been working with a group of men to compel certain landlords to make the tenement-houses they owned sanitary. Together these men had also been securing the enforcement of the law against certain infamous dens of vice which were a constant menace to the morals of the poor boys and girls who lived in the vicinity. They had been accomplishing something in securing employment for men out of work, for it was during the era of hard times. They had succeeded in securing, through a free market, a cheaper and more wholesome food supply for the poor. They had been coöperating in the work of a certain Social Settlement which supervises a number of boys' clubs and sewing-schools and working-men's resorts, bringing cheer and hope to hundreds of neglected lives. He had found a deep satisfaction in the part he had taken in it all, and as he concluded his narrative, he leaned across the table and said to me with the utmost earnestness: " You know I get nearer my Lord in working with those struggling people down there than I ever do in our church prayer-meeting." He was a man who could and did take an effective hand in the church prayer-meeting, too, but he had found his way into a deeper realization of the divine Spirit in his unselfish service to the needs of that section of the city, than in the usual conventional efforts after spirituality. Inasmuch as ye have sympathetically and helpfully known the least of these, ye have known Him!

As a matter of fact, the best men in the churches to-day are not trying to gain that deeper experience of the divine life which they crave by any mystical contemplation of the wounds of Christ until, like the saint of old, they have red spots in their hands; nor are they seeking it by endless striving for exact and final statements in dogma nor by painstaking attention to the minute details of ritual or polity, nor by fiery struggles for personal peace and safety. They are rather seeking the deeper realization of the Spirit of God through those activities which have to do with making good the claim, "We are all members one of another," thus coming into deeper fellowship with the Father of the whole household. When Christian people rightly relate their efforts for the establishment of justice, mercy, and peace in the associated life of men, to the purpose and Spirit of God, they will gain, in generous measure, that sane, warm and reliable spirituality which many current attempts are failing to secure.

If the churches should allow the trades-union to absorb the main part of the social energy of the community and the fraternal lodge to absorb the main part of its social sympathy, we should lose the whole divine treasure hidden in that fertile field. But if we can, changing the figure, recognize the presence of that social interest which knocks steadily at the door of the school and the magazine, the senate chamber and the church, as a divine presence; if we can hear its voice and interpret it aright; and if, still further, we can open the door, cordially admitting it to our fellowship and indicating our readiness to go with it on errands of useful service, we shall then sup indeed with the divine Author of that social interest and He with us, in a fuller realization of the kingdom of God on earth.

I have spoken thus far of the necessity which is, I believe, upon the churches, but the need of competent leadership is no less great from the point of view of those whose main interest is material betterment. There is a disposition in certain quarters to carry on the struggle as though enlightened and far-seeing self-interest would at last be sufficient to secure the well-being of the contending classes. And to those men who have lived under the unquestioned reign

of the Manchester School, there is a great need that
the law of Christ should be preached in place of that
iron law of wages. So long as certain employers,
consulting solely their own interest, will pay the
lowest wages which men can be induced to take; so
long as they will discharge men with families when
they find they can get boys and girls cheaper, without ever asking themselves what is to become of those
families; so long as they continue to attract to the
neighborhood where their industries are located great
numbers of cheap laborers, as was done by the coal
operators in Pennsylvania, knowing that they, by
the weight of their competing necessities, will force
down wages—so long as such narrow and immoral
self-interest holds undisputed sway, there can be no
permanent advance made toward the realization of
the kingdom of God, or of that industrial stability
even, which is an important element in the kingdom
of God.

And it is equally true that wherever union men
resort to terrorism and violence in order to coerce
those who differ with them in their industrial methods; wherever they insist upon having the final decision as to the discharge of employés for the payment of whose wages other men are responsible;
wherever they demand that factories, which the
brains and enterprise and capital of other men have

equipped and set in motion, shall be virtually controlled by themselves alone; wherever they insist that
no distinction shall be made in pay between efficient
and inefficient workmen; wherever they unduly close
the avenue to honorable industry for apprentices
wishing to learn a trade; wherever they break con-
tracts made and signed in times of peace, because of
a wish to coerce some other set of employers through
a sympathetic strike—they by their own acts also
retard the solution of the grave problem which rests
heavily upon them under modern conditions.   The
trades-unions, numbering their millions of members,
have other millions of toilers below them, for whom
they often seem to care not at all, and whose struggle
they make more difficult.   In this imperfect outlook
the union men themselves often become narrow, selfish, and despotic.

From both camps, then, there comes up a cry for
a larger habit of mind which shall look steadily, not
merely upon its own things, but also upon the things
of others.   Some men must be brought to see that
it would not advance the general prosperity to make
employés sole masters of the entire situation, thus
compelling capital and skill to take what might be
allowed them.   The very fact that the ability and
enterprise of others are in control might serve to indicate to the manual laborers that it is more than

possible that the same capacity which has given to its possessor that preëminence, may also possess some particular efficiency for the conduct of the enterprise. And some other men must be made to face the fact that no rich man ever becomes rich without the co-operation of many other men who give the best of their lives to the enterprise he has organized; and that all talk about " a man's right to manage his own business in his own way," regardless of the bearing of the industrial conditions maintained upon the health, the happiness, and the morals of these other men whose very lives are bound up in that bundle of prosperity with his own, is both irrational and immoral. His right to purchase labor does not include any sort of right to purchase the permanent and inevitable degradation of the laborer himself. And thus to purchase labor in the cheapest market, even though it does involve the sure degradation of the laborer and the destruction of all the possibilities of a wholesome family life for him, is as openly immoral as murder or adultery.

The people who have the sunny rooms in the social structure sometimes fail to get the point of view of those whose more meagre abilities have doomed them to the north side or possibly to a dark corner in the cellar. These fortunate people have accustomed themselves to " eat the fat and drink the sweet," with little or no disturbing consciousness of the needs of those for whom no adequate portion has been prepared, until the existing arrangement, inequitable though it may be, seems to them like the divine order. And because of this unmindful habit which springs out of that satisfying sense of comfort, there is call for the prophet to cry aloud at this point. It was that same deep sense of physical comfort on the part of the man who was warmly tucked into bed, who dreaded an excursion through a dark house to the larder, with the attendant fear of waking the baby, which led him to say to his needy neighbor: " Trouble me not; the door is now shut, and my children are with me in bed; I cannot rise and give thee." The very contentment bred of abundant possessions and a high degree of material comfort frequently dulls the cry of need outside and deadens the sense of social responsibility in those who are thus wrapped about with luxury.

That particular type of social responsibility which prompts generous gifts in charity when the need has become desperate, or handsome benefactions to homes and hospitals to care for the unhappy people who are maimed and broken in the battle of life, or vast endowments for public libraries where the unemployed, along with the rest, may spend their vacant hours more contentedly, or royal endowments for schools, which shall thereby be tempted at least to apologize for the existing order and to speak softly sometimes regarding social injustice in the methods of accumulating the gigantic fortunes whose benefactions they receive—that type of social responsibility may have some useful function to fulfil, but it does not reach far enough to possess any considerable utility. There is a strong demand that men shall be shown the moral bearing of their acts in those methods by which they accumulate their wealth. It was a true word which President Roosevelt spoke at the last Harvard Commencement. " It is far more important that rich men should conduct their business affairs decently than that they should spend the surplus of their fortunes in philanthropy." When certain industrial methods tend constantly to roll up, as they undoubtedly do, a perpetual supply of cripples and paupers, of unemployed and desperate men, they cannot surely be pronounced " decent " by an instructed conscience. Honest regard for the well-being of others must reach back and deal with the causes of distress more than with the results which are turned out at the other end of the system.

The application of intelligence and experience, under the skilful guidance of our own Luther Burbank, in California, to those fields of effort where the natural forces operate among the fruit and the flowers, has brought vastly superior returns. This has come about mainly through the blending of different forms of life by cross-fertilization. A similar application of intelligence and conscience to the fields of industrial effort will be still more rewarding. If there can be some cross-fertilization of the practical sagacity of the men of affairs who have done so much to produce this marvellous material development of recent years, with the spiritual vision and social sympathy of the prophet and the seer, it will mean a rich harvest of human values; it will mean an order of life which will not, on the one hand, be sordid and gross, or, on the other, shadowy and unreal. The nobler order thus to be realized would be indeed the new Jerusalem descending out of heaven from God, bringing its own divine method and spirit with it, but resting solidly upon the earth and gathering its materials from the common instincts and impulses of humanity. And in the great task of bringing this consummation nearer, there is sore need of competent, far-seeing, trustworthy leaders able to voice the social message from on high in the language in which the age was born and with which it carries on its eager and varied life.

Society can do what it ought to do—this I believe because I believe in the human will, finite but powerful. And what ought to be will be—this I believe because I believe in God, whose will is infinite and all powerful, as well as holy and benevolent. And because society has this power to create such a life as will genuinely express this will of God concerning it, we may depend upon those instincts which are resident within all the fairer aspects of society to respond to that leadership which can effectively and winsomely point the way. We are warranted in reposing a profound confidence in these subtle but invincible spiritual forces which can be aroused to action, and, when once aroused, can be organized and directed in such a way that all oppression and injustice must finally give way before their resistless advance.

The feeling that all the people who mean well are competent to undertake to set the world right has largely passed. The only men who can long gain a responsive hearing to-day are men who indicate clearly that they have studied their subject and that in some measure they are trained specialists touching the matter immediately in hand. The very nature of these social problems demands a high degree of efficiency in those who would undertake their solution. Neither individual nor social well-being ever grows wild. They grow only as the right seed is sown in the right way and in soil which has been suitably prepared in advance. When these conditions of a harvest are intelligently met, then, and only then, is it the will of God to give that increase of general well-being which the hungry heart of the world is craving.

It lies within the power of the American people to actually furnish this necessary efficiency for the solution of these problems. A Benjamin's portion of the brain power and the will power of our nation has thus far been given to the creation of a material fabric which clothes the favored classes in America with a prosperity unmatched before in all the history of the world. The hour has certainly come to now devote a larger share of this brain power and will power to the exaltation and the visible embodiment of certain spiritual ideals in this abundant life of ours. Commercial enterprise has absorbed unduly the strength and enthusiasm of our young manhood, and now there is a call for these younger sons of the covenant to bring forth more generously the moral leadership which they are well able to furnish, and to come up to the help of the Lord against the mighty and selfish materialism of the age.

When a prominent Christian minister, regarded as exceedingly conservative in all his views, formerly the pastor of a large and wealthy church in our chief city, can write such words as these, " The signs of the times admonish us that if Christianity is to avert a revolution of the most gigantic proportions and the most ruinous results, we have not an hour to lose in assuring the restless masses that they have no better friends than the disciples of Him whose glory it was to preach good tidings to the poor and to lift their grievous burdens," it is surely in order for all ministers to strive to see clearly, to speak sanely, and to help actively in the solution of these grave social problems. In some way the people of our land must learn, if we are to have peace and safety, not only how to produce abundantly, but at the same time to distribute justly and to consume rationally. The first has been mastered by the American mind; the last two await a more truly social conscience enthroned in the heart. The strong and successful have learned the full meaning of American independence—they must now be brought to discover the full significance of the obligations which go with interdependence in this close-knit life of our modern world. They must be brought by the ministers of Jesus Christ to realize that " the head cannot say to the foot," the highest in ability cannot say to the lowest, " I have no need of you," but that all are members one of another in a common responsibility, in a general care of all for each and of each for all.

The day has passed when it was permissible for any man haughtily to assert his right " to run his

own business in his own way" or to spend his own
money as he pleased. It passed, indeed, a long time
ago from the Christian point of view. Ambrose, the
Bishop of Milan, a man of affairs who had accumulated a fortune and served with honor as governor
of the province before he became a priest, thus defined the truly Christian attitude away back in the
fourth century. " My own business! " he says, echo-
ing the selfish claim of some man who had asserted
a similarly exclusive right. " What injustice is
there, you ask, in my diligently preserving my own,
so long as I do not invade the property of others?
Shameless saying! *My own!* What is it? From
what sacred place hast *thou* brought it into the world?
Thou who hast received the gifts of God, thinkest
thou that thou committest no injustice in keeping
for thyself alone what would be the means of life to
many? It is the bread of the hungry thou keepest;
it is the clothing of the naked thou lockest up;
the money thou buriest is the redemption of the
wretched." The famous bishop thus voiced for his
time and for all time the sense of obligation which
ought to attach to the ownership of property, to the
control of industrial enterprises, and to all those
forms of influence which bear upon the welfare of
one's fellows.

We have, indeed, science enough—political, sanitary, economic, and ethical science—to point the way toward a freeing of the world from the greater portion of its disease and crime, its poverty and distress; but we have not conscience enough or good will enough to apply fearlessly and hopefully what we already know along these lines. The blessing promised in those great words of Christ, " If ye know these things, happy are ye if ye do them," still waits upon the readiness of men to translate knowledge into action. The most imperative need, therefore, is not so much for further instruction in the actual facts which make up these problems, as for those mighty spiritual influences which may be brought to bear in such a way as effectively to stimulate the action of the will in doing that which the clear eye already sees to be right.

Many of you who are gathered here to-day in this seminary are to minister in the Congregational churches of this country. It would be in the line of a genuine " apostolic succession " if some of you should come to be enrolled with the pioneers in this work of furnishing moral leadership for the social struggle which is to have so large a place in the life to which you will be called to minister. Your predecessors, the Puritan pastors of New England, were strong in their sense of the new social order which was to come as the earthly realization of the kingdom of God. They dreamed of a genuine theocracy, a civil order in which the reign of the divine Spirit would be complete. However imperfect and even clumsy modern criticism may deem some of their attempts to establish their social ideals, the real content of those ideals, the brave conception of an associated life which should embody and express the will and purpose of God for men, was possessed of high and lasting value. And it will add a hundred-fold to your own usefulness as pastors if you, too, may, in the language of your day, hold aloft ideals which shall be equally commanding, and labor for their realization with the same splendid zeal.

CHAPTER II

It would be difficult to name any other serious work in all the world of useful activity which is commonly done in quite such haphazard fashion as is the work of religious instruction from the average pulpit. The moment the minister finishes his breakfast on Tuesday morning he realizes that next Sunday is coming. While he was attending the ministers' meeting the day before, and otherwise beguiling the time, that oft-recurring day of judgment has been gaining on him—it has already passed the first of the six short laps which lie between him and his next public appearance in the pulpit. " What shall I preach on next Sunday ? " he is constrained to ask himself. And ordinarily he is free to preach on anything in heaven above or in the earth beneath, or in that other place, the precise location and character of which are not quite so clearly understood to-day as they once were, acccording to their claim, by some of our theological predecessors.

If this minister is nothing but a timeserver and an opportunist he may decide to wait a day or two

and see what the ravens, that is, the newspapers, may
bring him in the way of some sensation or some
startling question of the hour, which will furnish
him "a drawing theme." There are misguided
prophets sitting by all the brooks Cherith which flow,
hungry for some such ready-made topic and intent
upon the columns of the daily press for some morsel
which may be thus hastily served up as a sermon.
The minister may, if he chooses, seize upon that new
idea which came to him in last week's reading; or
he may decide to give a few individual sinners, whose
personal shortcomings have loomed before him con-
spicuously within the last few days, their meat in
due season; or he may simply follow some whim or
mood, taking any theme which appeals to him most
strongly at that particular moment; or he may act
upon the counsel given him in the seminary, ask for
the direct guidance of the Holy Ghost in the selection of his topic.

This last endeavor, if he is led to make it, is
beyond all criticism and is, indeed, an imperative
duty for every prophet of the living God. But you
will find as you go along, brethren, that such specific
guidance by the Holy Spirit, sought for and expected
on the spot, is a very difficult thing to gain; and,
perhaps, still harder to be definitely recognized when
gained—as some one has said, " only with great care

and discernment to be distinguished from a lot of other impulses which look much like it at times." And you will also come to see increasingly that " the Holy Spirit is a very wise and orderly Spirit," with abundant reasons lying back for all that He does and for all that He impels His confused and hesitating followers to do; and, furthermore, that His particular guidance is granted us all the more surely and helpfully if we already have some sensible and scriptural habits in the selection of our themes for the work of the pulpit. As a matter of fact, the Lord will lead us, very much as He did Abraham's servant, when that ancient worthy sought divine guidance along with the constant exercise of the utmost good judgment which he himself possessed in regard to a certain matter—" I being in the way, the Lord led me."

All of the foregoing methods by which men vault suddenly into the sadddle of some theme and ride it hastily into the pulpit on the following Sunday are open to serious objection, and I would urge upon you, therefore, the wisdom of adopting some wiser plan. Your stray choices, springing out of your own dominant and oft-recurring moods, are liable to over-specialize you and to get you into the way of playing all your Gospel music on two or three stops, whereas the congregation has a right to hear the full organ, swell, choir, pedal, great organ and all, sixty stops, if you are personally capable of being brought to such richness. The congregation has a right to hear you with everything turned on—all the stops that are within you blessing the Lord and sounding out the full harmony of the Gospel in its many notes. If you should become thus over-specialized and narrowed down into a jews-harp, your people would suffer loss, and many of them would gradually drop away to other sanctuaries, where a full organ still led the worship and shaped the aspiration of the congregation.

I am therefore a firm believer in well-constructed courses of sermons, which give the advantage of some useful system at least to pulpit instruction. The orderly lessons of the Church Year in the prayer book, with the habit of selecting the text from the Gospel or the Epistle for the day, is a wholesome arrangement and tends to save the preachers in the Episcopal Church from partial views of truth and from ill-timed flightiness. It may not be expedient for all ministers in this bustling period to march with measured tread through the stately ongoings of that Church Year, but order can be had, plentiful and beautiful, outside of any such prescribed arrangement.

I have used for some years, with growing satisfac-

tion to myself and with increased interest and profit
secured to my congregation, the method of expository
preaching, devoting at certain seasons months and
months together to the exposition of single books in
the Bible. I wish here to indicate strongly my sense
of the value of this method and to speak of its special
appropriateness and utility in presenting that social
message which is my main theme.

Personally I have found it best to announce no
programme or schedule in advance—the Gospel Train
does not need to run as yet with all the minute
exactness of a " Twentieth Century Limited." I use
the book in hand for the morning or for the evening
service, as the particular passage for that day may
be best adapted to the differing congregations. I
hold it easily, so that it can be dropped for a Sunday
on occasion, if Christmas, Palm Sunday, or Easter,
or if the presentation of some benevolent cause and
the taking of an offering should intervene. I select
such a portion of the book as will best lend itself to
topical treatment, sometimes a whole chapter or more,
sometimes a half or a third of a chapter—we cannot
cut off the several portions we intend to serve up to
our people as " meat that endureth," according to
any hard-and-fast rule. And in this way in my
present pastorate, where I have been for ten years,
I have already preached six months each, in three

different years, on Matthew, Mark, and Luke; six
months on the Book of Acts; six months on First
and Second Corinthians; three months on Genesis,
three months on Exodus and four months on Joshua,
with other courses of sermons on Job, on Isaiah, and
on the Minor Prophets.

You will find that some people will enjoy this style
of preaching from the outset; many more can be
quickly taught to enjoy it, and those who, perhaps,
turn away from such simple, scriptural fare can have
their wants supplied at the other service—or, possibly, by some church across the way. It was never
meant that any one lone man should expect to preach
with equal acceptance and effectiveness to all creation
—such a thing would spoil him with conceit and be
unfair to his fellow-pastors besides. Your sheep
will hear your voice, for by your particular style of
preaching you will gradually call out their names
and their needs, and they will follow you. And even
while you are striving to make your own flock as
large as maybe, you will rejoice continually over the
other sheep which are not of your fold—the other
sheep which the Lord is bringing along by a style
of ministry that you could not possibly furnish. It
is by virtue of this varied appeal that they, too, will
be brought to hear and heed the call of that Good
Shepherd who is over all the flocks.

When you undertake to preach for a series of months on a certain book in the Bible, you do not, to borrow a felicitous figure of speech used by Dr. Nathaniel J. Burton, " snatch out a text and carry it off as a dog might carry off a likely looking bone," in order to ascertain what meat you can pick off for your people. You take the whole book, with all its layers of fat and tenderloin; you sit down with it for prolonged interviews and for many wholesome, satisfying meals. By the use of spiritual imagination you set before your mind the whole period in which that book originally took shape, with its speech and manners and all its belongings, as a live section of the world's experience which you propose to interpret and utilize in the work of spiritual instruction for half a year or more. You lay in a stock of books and commentaries bearing upon that particular portion of Holy Scripture. You keep up this persistent and systematic study week after week, until you know as much about that book in the Bible as it is possible for a man of your size to know. And then reverting to our figure again, you cut off, from Sunday to Sunday, such roasts and joints as can be most acceptably served up, to feed your people, not as with the meat that perisheth, but with that meat which endureth unto everlasting life. This form of spiritual nourishment may indeed be termed

" meat which the Son of man has given you "—
given you in all the more generous and satisfying
measure because of your diligent effort thus systematically to receive it at His hands. I regard this
as the finest form of orderliness possible to those of
us who work in non-ritualistic churches. In the
course of any well-rounded-out pastorate, you can
see what systematic training the people would thus
receive in wholesome Scripture interpretation, and
what a wide and inspiring acquaintance they would
gain with all the great truths of religion and of life
from the biblical standpoint.

It not only rounds out a man's ministry, but it
enables him to say a great many homely and useful
things which he might not find it natural to say were
he pursuing the plan of preaching nothing but topical sermons. The entire Bible fits in around the
total human need like a well-made suit of clothes.
There is no sin or sorrow, no doubt or difficulty, no
temptation or duty which is not contemplated and
provided for somewhere within its ample folds. The
man who is following its lead will therefore be certain to discover all the manifold needs of his people,
and soon or late to bring something to the aid of
each one in the course of such extended expository
work.

It also enables the minister to speak plainly and

directly touching certain sins which show their ugly
heads in the lives of some of the very people before
him, without any suspicion whatever of going out
of his way to rap their individual knuckles. This
last is the meanest of all pulpit sins—to take an unfair advantage of some individual, where the usages
of public worship and all the proprieties of the occasion forbid his talking back, in order to vent one's
spite upon him and to say what one might hesitate
to say in a personal interview. I trust none of you
will ever stoop to that. Whenever you want to say
" Thou art the man," have the good sense to imi-
tate Nathan's method as well as his boldness, by
seeking out the offender when he is alone.

In the exposition of such a book as Matthew's Gospel, for example: the Sermon on the Mount, with its
picture of a social condition where right-minded and
honest-hearted men would no longer live under a
constant, harassing anxiety as to what they should
eat and what they should drink and wherewithal they
should be clothed; the Saviour's call to the weary
and the heavy laden, who, by coming unto Him, in
all that this implies, both for the individual and for
the corporate life of the race, were to find that to
which they and their fathers had been strangers—
" rest unto their souls "; the series of parables touching that kingdom which is destined to transform

common life as with a new leaven, and to reorganize it as a beautiful tree; the sad picture of able-bodied men eager to work, but standing all day idle in the market-place because no man had hired them; the pathetic story of men wearily bearing the heat and burden of exhausting toil for a penny a day; the lessons of social responsibility unfolded in the failure of the foolish virgins, in the action of the man who hoarded his talent instead of investing it in useful service, and, above all, in that sublime judgment scene where final acceptance or rejection at the hands of the Judge of all the earth turns upon the way men have dealt with the hungry and the needy, the sick and the imprisoned—all these passages in that one gospel, standing along the way of his pulpit ministrations like open doors, will compel the man who is preaching a series of expository sermons on that book to speak out many a plain word on social righteousness which shall be to his listeners as a gospel for the day.

In the systematic exposition of Matthew also, it will not only be natural, it will be inevitable that the preacher, with Christ's words before him, should declare plainly what he believes to be the whole counsel of God in regard to marriage and divorce, even though certain well-dressed pew-holders who have put away their wives through the hardness of their hearts, replacing them with more attractive substitutes, should sit uneasily in their places. With that twenty-third chapter of Matthew standing solidly in his way as he moves through the book, he must also speak plainly against that wicked hypocrisy which prays long prayers in its patient and regular attendance upon the services of the sanctuary, and then pays the pew-rent, perhaps, with profits derived from devouring widows' houses by the commercial methods which rule its actions during the intervening six days. He will also be prompted, by Christ's straightforward utterance, to discuss carefully the reasons for that unnatural and unholy compulsion of multitudes of our fellow-beings to be " anxious " as to " what they shall eat and drink and what they shall put on "—anxious from the dawning of the sense of responsibility for their own support, until they are laid away, it may be, in the potter's field. He will have a straight word to say to those who, in the face of Christ's own positive declaration, still believe that somehow they can serve both God and Mammon by simply appointing different days for the respective efforts, dividing the time in the ratio of six to one, with the long end of the bargain in favor of Mammon. With such a passage as this awaiting exposition, " I have compassion on the multitude because they continue with me now three days and have noth-

ing to eat: and I will not send them away fasting,
lest they faint in the way," the preacher will inevitably urge the obligation of a widely inclusive
social sympathy; from the passage which opens with
the statement, " It is easier for a camel to go through
the eye of a needle than for a rich man to enter into
the kingdom of God," he will make plain the difficulty
of holding and administering large possessions in a
thoroughly Christian way, a difficulty which every
conscientious rich man to-day, when the moral aspects of the methods of accumulation are being closely scrutinized, is coming to fully recognize; with that
picture of men neglecting the supreme things in life
because of their very absorption in " farms " and
in " merchandise," the minister will openly rebuke
the same wretched tendency which is a moral menace
to our age.   These sample passages, all of them taken
from that single book, serve, in their bearing upon
many of the social problems and evils of our own
day, to indicate the splendid opportunities which thus
open to an expository preacher who is desirous of
delivering a social message to his own times as an
organic part of the eternal evangel.

Or the minister might undertake the exposition of
that brief but exceedingly instructive Book of James.
The scorn which the modern world justly heaps upon
the religious profession which fails to utter itself

in a steadfast effort to perform the duties which that profession involves, is here declared in words that burn. The essential elements of " pure and unde-filed religion " are here most accurately defined as holiness and usefulness, the keeping of the life un-spotted from the world and the investment of it in service rendered to the fatherless and the widows as types of the world's need. The unseemly eagerness of some churches to enjoy the good-will of the fortu-nate, saying to the man with goodly apparel and the gold ring, " Sit thou here," and to the poor man in vile raiment, " Stand thou there," comes in for ef-fective rebuke. The wickedness of reckless speech in public address, in the columns of the press, in the unthinking utterances of many an agitator, is here set out in clear type: The tongue is called " a wild beast which no man can tame "; the tongue is ' a fire kindled from the fire of hell '; the tongue is ' a little member but able to defile the whole body ' of one's influence; the tongue is the most effective instrument we possess for good or ill—" therewith bless we God even the Father and therewith curse we men . . . out of the same mouth proceed blessing and cursing." The spiritual indifference and the in-solent defiance of the divine claims upon us, exhibited by those who say, " To-day or to-morrow we will go into such a city and continue there a year, and buy and sell and get gain," not knowing where they will be on the morrow, because the life they live is " a vapor that appeareth for a little time and then vanisheth away "—this whole attitude, which is as modern as an automobile, is here brought face to face with its ugly self and with its deleterious influence! The riches which are " corrupted " at their source by the methods employed in gaining them; the gold and silver which is " cankered " by the stains which injustice and oppression had left upon its possessors; the all too meagre " hire of laborers " who reaped down the fields, but whose rightful reward is " kept back " by fraud; the irresponsible conduct of those who " live in pleasure " on the earth, but are " wanton " in their lack of any true sense of obligation—all these forms of evil-doing in modern society inevitably come in for treatment by the man who would give his congregation a series of expository sermons on the Book of James.

Or, if the minister should turn to the Old Testament and undertake the systematic exposition of the First Isaiah, he would find himself in possession of abundant and useful material for a social message to his own times. " Woe unto them that decree unrighteous decrees to turn aside the needy from judgment and to take away the right from the poor of my people," he could cry in the language of this early prophet! He could say just that, with the modern accent upon it, to the ruthless managers of great corporate interests who often trample upon the rights of laborers, and upon the small, independent operators, and upon the helpless public, by manipulating not only prices and markets, but the common carriers and the courts, and even the legislatures, for their own gain. In the face of showy worship, costly churches and ostentatious gifts to ecclesiastical enterprises accompanied by social injustice, the minister could say with Isaiah: "To what purpose is the multitude of your sacrifices unto me? Bring no more vain oblations; incense is an abomination unto me! Who hath required this at your hands? Your new moons and your appointed feasts my soul hateth. But put away the evil of your doings from before mine eyes! Seek judgment, relieve the oppressed; judge the fatherless; plead for the widow." Against the hot-headed enthusiasts who mistake jingoism for patriotism, and against those who recklessly foment international differences, thus secretly encouraging the habit of war because of the stimulus it offers to certain lines of business, he could hurl the words of the prophet: "The Lord shall judge among the nations and shall rebuke many people: and they shall beat their swords into ploughshares, and their spears into pruning-hooks"; they shall convert the destructive forces into productive ones, utilizing the bright metal of the nation's young manhood not to destroy but to sustain men's lives. He could sing of the time when "nation shall not lift up sword against nation, neither shall they learn war any more."

In this Book of Isaiah, also, the current materialism, operating not as a philosophical doctrine but as a social tendency, is most effectively rebuked. 'Their land is full of silver and gold, neither is there any end of their treasures. Their land is also full of horses, neither is there any end of their chariots. Their land is also full of idols; they worship the work of their own hands, that which their own fingers have made.' The alarming readiness of the strong and the shrewd cruelly to exploit for their own advantage the labor of the weak, and their willingness to crush out the chance of progress for the people of small means, come in for a stern condemnation where the prophet discerning the same tendency in his own day, cries: 'The Lord will enter into judgment with His people, for ye have eaten up the vineyard; the spoil of the poor is in your houses. What mean ye that ye beat my people to pieces, and grind the faces of the poor, saith the Lord of Hosts?' The menacing figure of selfish monopoly, holding itself superior to the law and disregarding the interests of the consuming public, which stalks through our own Republic unashamed, is here held up to scorn in those ringing words: ' Woe unto them that join house to house and lay field to field until there be no room, that they may dwell alone in the midst of the earth. He looked for justice but behold oppression, for righteousness but behold a cry.' The sophists of the press and the chair and the pulpit, the special pleaders, the perverters of truth and right, the specious defenders of the social wrong-doing which has brought a blight upon modern civilization and lowered the moral tone of the nation are thus arraigned: ' Woe unto them that call evil good and good evil; that put darkness for light and light for darkness; that put bitter for sweet and sweet for bitter.' And all those who would make the social struggle a contest of brute force for material advantage, who believe that our deliverance and safety can be gained altogether by physical power and legal might, no attention whatever being given to that unseen Spirit, who is not far from any one of us—all those mistaken souls will find wholesome instruction in that solemn passage: " Woe to them that go down to Egypt for help, that stay on horses and trust in chariots because they are many, but look not unto the Holy One of Israel neither seek the Lord. The Egyptians are men and not God, their horses are flesh and not spirit. Turn ye therefore unto Him from whom ye have deeply revolted." Thus spoke the leading prophet of Israel in the eighth century before Christ, to the social conditions of his own land and time; and thus he speaks with those notes of divine truth which are timeless, regarding the problems we are called upon to face in this twentieth century after Christ.

I will not further multiply illustrations of the value and pertinency of whole sections of Scripture in thus furnishing the best of all bases for the word of the modern prophet to the social conditions of his own time. I have here quoted these many passages from Matthew, from James, and from Isaiah, not as carefully selected proof-texts in support of my contention—such a use of the Bible has come to be largely discredited, for the simple reason that by plucking single passages out of the context here and there, and by cleverly piecing them together in the interests of some particular theory, the most extravagant and unwarranted propositions can be given an apparent support from Scripture. I have cited these many and varied passages rather to indicate how strong and how clear was the social interest and sympathy of the men whose utterances are here recorded; how plain it was to them that the recovery of the social life from the abuses which had fastened upon it was an essential part of the task of religion; and how effectively they grappled with the moral values bound up with these social problems, as is indicated by the fact that the main principles of their message are just as applicable to our own situation as they were to the needs of those who were immediately addressed.

The social message from God to men, as outlined in the Bible, is in no sense, then, an aside or a by-product; it is not incidental to the main purpose of the Gospel, but an essential part of it. The redemption proposed was not merely to bring men up to the point where they would love God with all their hearts, it was to establish them as well in that real and abiding love for their neighbors which would show itself in a justly organized and equitably administered social life. In seeking, therefore, to make the every-day life of men, with its network of social relations consuming the bulk of their strength and interest, a real habitation of the Spirit, a temple of the living God wherein the souls of His children may dwell all the days of their lives—Sunday, Monday, Tuesday, Wednesday, and all the rest, beholding steadily in their secular experiences the beauty of the Lord and strengthened constantly by the sense of exalted fellowship—in seeking to bring the organized life of modern society up to that high ideal, the minister of the Gospel is not a stranger or a foreigner; he is a fellow-citizen with the saints and of the household of God; he is, in all that high endeavor, building directly upon the foundation of the prophets and apostles, Jesus Christ Himself being the chief corner-stone!

We may say, then, that not only does the preacher find abundant material for a social message ready to his hand in the Scripture; not only is he permitted and encouraged to address himself directly to the consideration of these problems by the example of those inspired men who have preceded him in the age-long task of human redemption—the social teachings of the Bible are so fundamental to the whole approach it makes to our necessities, that there is an imperative call for that type of preaching. The minister who should give his main strength to the inculcation of a personal and private piety in that little group of souls to which he might devote himself, leaving out of view the rightful articulation of those lives to the industrial and political framework in which they stand, would be unfaithful to the high commission he had received. The modern apostles, no less than the original twelve, are sent out to preach, saying, " The kingdom of heaven is at hand." And it is plain to every intelligent man that the ideal society here proposed can only be at hand, even potentially and prospectively, where the readjustment of social relations according to the spirit and method announced by Christ is steadily kept in view as a vital part of the work of regeneration.

It was an American bishop of a former generation, standing in the true apostolic succession, not by virtue of any peculiar title-deeds held by his own communion, but through his own high character and noble usefulness, who said: " More than once did the Hebrew kings seek to break away from the intermeddling of the clergy, but God smote the politician and not the prophet. Saul meddled with Samuel's duties and God took his kingdom from him; but Samuel was never censured for his intermeddling with the affairs of Saul. David had to submit to the authority of more than one priest or prophet, but no prophet was ever compelled to silence before him. Isaiah, Ezekiel, Jeremiah, Amos, Hosea, and all the preachers of righteousness dwelt on social and civic sins—they dwelt on hardly anything else." The man who proclaims his social message, therefore, both in the terms and in the spirit of the best Scripture the world has, will be made strong by the reënforcement which comes from his sense of coöperation with that spirit of righteousness manifest in the work of the saints and seers, the prophets and apostles of all time, that spirit of righteousness which is from everlasting to everlasting.

The sublime sense of responsibility for the interests of the child, for example, which the Bible habitually manifests, will furnish the Christian preacher a noble foundation for his opposition to the present disgraceful and menacing custom of exploiting childhood for gain. " Whoso shall cause one of these little ones which believe in me to stumble, it were better for him that a mill-stone were hanged about his neck and that he were drowned in the depth of the sea." " Take heed that ye despise not one of these little ones, for I say unto you that in heaven their angels do always behold the face of my Father, which is in heaven." " It is not the will of your Father which is in heaven that one of these little ones should perish." This is the great word of Christ Himself, and how wickedly we have sinned against it here and there in modern industry by the greedy use of the profitable labor of immature children!

The Child Labor Law of Pennsylvania forbids the employment of boys in the coal mines under the age of sixteen, and in the breakers or about the mines under the age of fourteen years. But Dr. Peter Roberts, in his book " The Anthracite Coal Communities," estimates that there are in the anthracite region not less than six thousand four hundred boys under the age of fourteen employed in and about the mines, basing his estimate on personal investigation and the statistics of certain sections of the district collected at first hand. Owen R. Lovejoy, in a group of twenty-two breaker boys, found from examination of the school record, showing their former attendance, that one was nine, four were ten, two were eleven, six were twelve, three were thirteen years of age— sixteen out of twenty-two were under fourteen and were therefore employed in violation of the law of the State. " For nine hours a day these little fellows toil in the breaker, bending over a stream of coal which pours out a cloud of dust so thick that the light cannot penetrate it. They are responsible for the exact separation from the coal of all slate and rock —depending often entirely on the sense of touch. They endure the incessant rattle of deafening, gigantic machinery. They suffer the stifling heat of summer at one season and the bitter blasts that sweep these mountain-tops at another. They are conscious that the ' boss ' stands behind with his stick or a small piece of coal to prompt to duty if the natural exuberance of childhood breaks out in playfulness or if backache induces a moment of forgetfulness. They have their hands cut and crippled and hardened by contact with the rough stones and bits of sharp-edged coal. They must learn to control the nausea caused by swallowing quantities of coal-dust and by the feeling that one's throat and lungs are never

clean! These are experiences which it may still be
necessary for stalwart men to endure in order to
provide society with this staple; but to bare the tender
body of a boy of nine or ten years to such a life, to
rob him of the too brief period of play-time and
growth by the hardening exactions of such a daily
routine, is to doom him to a gray monotony of unin-
spiring prospect from which all beauty, art, joy in
labor, and hope of better things are forever shut out."

And when we realize that all this is being done
because " business is business," because the appetites
of the stockholders in the mines are keen for big
dividends, thus impelling the superintendent to get
the work done as cheaply as possible, we wonder if
we are really living in a Christian country! We
wonder how we can sit at the glowing grate-fire and
not see therein the burned-out lives of little children
whose vitality has been withered and blasted in the
process of producing the coal! It was on behalf
of just such children as these that the sympathetic
heart of Christ spoke his words of warning. Woe
unto him that causeth one of these little ones to
stumble—it were better that a mill-stone were hanged
about his neck and that he were cast into the depths
of the sea.

The very fact that the minister of religion grounds
his social message in the Bible, drawing it organically

and vitally out of a regular course of scriptural instruction, relieves him from the charge, so readily
made against a man who has more to say about the
sins of the people before him than about the sins of
Jeroboam and Rehoboam, of being a sensationalist.
The scriptural quality of his message lifts it up and
gives it the quality of timelessness. It is, indeed, the
eternal evangel in its substance, and yet in its application it is as fresh and pertinent as this morning's
daily paper. This habit of expository preaching thus
fortifies the minister in his position; it tends to remove the prejudice which many people feel toward
preaching upon questions of the day, a prejudice
which sometimes closes the door against a helpful
message; and it lodges many disturbing but useful
lessons within the hearts of those who cannot put the
Bible out of the door, as they are sometimes tempted
to do with the minister whose sermon has made them
uncomfortable. Such lessons lovingly taught serve
to instruct them in the higher righteousness, to make
them wise unto a deeper salvation, and to furnish
them thoroughly for every good work.

There is also high value in attaching any important
truth to what is already familiar and beloved. In
the judgment of many men, the greatest asset, hu-
manly speaking, which the Episcopal Church has
is its Prayer-Book. The true Episcopalian might be

fittingly described in those words from the Book of Revelation, " He had in his hand a little book, open." The Prayer-Book is a little book; it can readily be held in any hand, open; it can be carried in the pocket, read on the train, held by the sick; it is a manual of devotion in every way portable and usable. It contains the Psalms, a selection from the Gospels, and another from the Epistles, for every Sunday in the year. It has in it some of the choicest words gleaned from the aspirations of the ages, prayers of every kind for " all sorts and conditions of men "—its Litany enfolds our whole range of spiritual need and carries it up as with the sense of a wide-spread and corporate fellowship of devotion, before the throne of the Universal Father. And the very fact that the service of worship in every Episcopal church, and the private devotions of the individual Christian, and the religious office at weddings, christenings, burials, are all attached to this familiar little book, adds to their effectiveness and to its effectiveness in ministering to the spiritual life.

In much more extended fashion the words of the Bible, its histories and biographies, its songs and prayers, its ethical appeals and spiritual visions, its words of promise, cheer, and comfort, as well as its unmistakable rebukes and warnings, its deep insights, broad outlooks, and profound revelations, have all found a place in the general consciousness of a large part of Christendom. And when the particular instruction needed for special interests and situations can be closely and warmly related to that body of literature and to the vaster body of sentiment which enfolds it, the value of the instruction is enhanced a hundred-fold. You can see at once the unspeakable advantage to be gained by attaching the social message closely and systematically to the instruction given in the Scriptures.

The Bible in its length and breadth, its heights and depths, is not a book mainly for the recluse. Those business men, living, as many of them do, with manifold burdens and anxieties; living, as many of them do, out on the frontier, where right and wrong meet face to face six days in the week and fight to the death; tempted, as many of them are, to sing the song of life in a lower key than it was ever meant to be pitched—they all need the helpful ministry of these pages of Scripture. They need habitual conference with a book which is not afraid of them as it calls upon them to stand up before the highest and most searching ideals, as it invites them to try conclusions with the purposes of God concerning them, as it seeks to bring them to know Him who stands ready to be the efficient guide and helper of their busy lives.

And those other men who do the rough work of the world in the mills and the mines, in the factories and in the foundries, in all the trades and crafts which take up the physical strength of the race, they need this entire book no less. They are tempted sometimes to make their social effort a mere brute struggle for material advantage. They listen to agitators and read trade journals, which sometimes fall into a way of speaking as if the wage-earner were only a superior kind of cab horse, intent solely upon shorter hours, a better barn, and more oats. All such agitation, as we know, is doomed to failure for lack of moral energy to carry it on and up; but those whose spiritual eyes are dull because of severe toil, and who are slow of heart to believe the good things which God has prepared for those who coöperate with Him, are often blinded to the larger issues at stake. If out of this book, which is not regarded as partisan or timeserving, out of this book which has come down through the ages as a divine messenger to preach good tidings to the poor, to bind up the broken-hearted, to preach deliverance to the captive, and to set at liberty them that are bruised, the appeal of the modern preacher may come, sharing in the wide and permanent sanction which attaches to its utterances, his words will be endued with power from on high.

However it came about, we have not thus far succeeded in rearing up Christian men and women in any considerable numbers who prove to be largely, nobly, and steadily useful, except as they have been fed, and well fed, on Scripture. The paper and the magazine, the religious poem and the sermon, may all come in, and they ought to come in, but there is still an unapproached primacy in the Scriptures themselves. They instruct men in righteousness, and furnish them thoroughly for all good work in a way that nothing else seems to have succeeded in doing. If, then, we are to have men of fine quality, large faith, moral vigor, bearing with them the sense and atmosphere of God's presence, and able to stand firm in every hour of trial, we must have men into whose spiritual fibre these ancient Scriptures have gone. Our main reliance in the work of spiritual progress will be upon that Christian consciousness which is saturated with Bible truth, instructed by the world-wide, age-long experience of the church, and applied to conduct by moral reason. And because of that dominant interest in social questions, which is at present the open door to many thousands of lives, it is of vital importance that the social message for our day should have this biblical basis.

The whole interpretation of ordinary life will be affected by this scriptural point of view. When the mind of a congregation comes to be thoroughly saturated with the language and the concepts of the four gospels, we will say, this will naturally and irresistibly infuse new meanings into many of the expressions of daily life. "How much is a certain man worth?" we often ask. Such a question will be given a new content and will receive a more complete reply when society has been trained to think in terms of Scripture. How much is he worth? Is he worth what he costs? Does he give value received in actual service rendered for what he takes of the common wealth? Is he worth feeding, clothing, and maintaining in the expensive way he has come to insist upon at the hands of society? All these considerations must be taken into account before we can reply as to how much he is worth.

How much is he worth? The ordinary reply is a statement of the value of his material possessions. This, however, does not tell us anything about the worth of the man—it simply states the price of the things that he possesses. But no man's life "consisteth in the abundance of the things that he possesseth"; it consists always in those qualities and capabilities which render him a useful member of society and an honored servant of the living God. The scriptural point of view, therefore, as it becomes habitual aids us in a just interpretation of all the terms and interests of common life.

In her volume on " Democracy and Social Ethics," Jane Adams, of Hull House, Chicago, indicates the different view-points of three persons who might look upon an eight-year-old boy who darts into a street-car selling evening papers. The well-to-do business man buys a paper from the little chap with no sense of moral repulsion—on the contrary, he may feel a certain satisfaction that he is helping an energetic boy to make his way in the world. The philanthropic lady next him thinks it a pity that such a bright boy should not be in school; she resolves to redouble her efforts on behalf of night-schools in the newsboys homes so that this child may have some chance at an education. The thoughtful working-man sitting opposite, trained in trades-union methods, sees the boy's natural development arrested by this abnormal activity, which uses up energy that should go into growth; he has seen men entering the factory at eighteen so worn out by premature work that they were laid on the shelf within ten or fifteen years; and so he regards the early use of this boy's powers as having but a momentary and specious value. He knows that while he may be able to do nothing for this particular boy, he can help agitate for child-labor laws, for the prohibition of street vending by children, so that the child of the poorest may have secured to him a chance for growth and education.

The view of the third man is the only view which embodies within it the spirit of social righteousness, kindly and well meant as may be the interest of the first two. But it is also necessary to see this boy as the men who wrote the Bible would have seen him. We must view him in his moral and spiritual possibilities in order to enlist powerfully on his behalf all the forces which are demanded for his proper nurture. To see in that boy a potential force in the kingdom of God, a son of the resurrection, an image of the divine likeness, and to see all these possibilities going down in defeat by his withdrawal from wholesome influences into the rough life of the street, and by the premature strain of unnatural labor—in a word, to see that boy as the men of the Bible would have seen him is to bring to bear another and still more powerful set of motives for his redemption.

The habit of grounding his social message in the Scriptures will, therefore, aid the preacher mightily in emphasizing those spiritual values which are at stake in the industrial struggle. The labor question is always more than an economic question, a struggle as to hours and wages—it is preëminently a spiritual question wherein the souls of men made in the likeness and image of God are at stake. Those peremptory notices " No admittance except on business " must come down—other weighty considerations, in no sense financial, must be permitted to enter into the determination of the courses of action which bear upon the conduct of all these enterprises. The question as to what are the profits of any business is a proper and a necessary one, but that other question, as to what kind of men and women the employés are becoming through the influences imposed upon them by the conditions of their toil, takes precedence over any question of profit. Sabatier has truly said, " Sociologists are more and more coming to the conclusion that the social question is dependent on the moral question; and that in order to secure the reign of justice and to bring about universal happiness, men must be taught to conquer selfishness and to love one another."

It is a universal *law* that men should bear one another's burdens—any effort to effect a permanent escape from that obligation is as futile as the effort to avoid the responsibilities imposed in the law of gravitation. It is a universal *law* that the strong should bear the infirmities of the weak, not allowing them to be crushed by disproportionate burdens— society must accept its life, if it is to continue to live at all, upon those terms. It is a universal *law* that we are all members one of another, knit up in a solidarity of interest extending from the least to the greatest and imposing duties which are coextensive with human existence. All this the Scripture makes so plain that these are but the commonplaces of Holy Writ. In phrasing his message in the terms of Scripture, therefore, the modern prophet will be delivered once for all from that snare of selfish materialism which is the weakness of many a modern social effort.

The very fact that Christendom, under the stimulus and guidance of these scriptural ideals, has made so much headway in its climb upward out of moral barbarism, indicates that when the social principles of the Gospel are still more bravely and thoroughly applied we shall be the joyous witnesses of a more splendid advance. " The fact that a ship is already a thousand miles at sea indicates that it will go farther." There are many things now which a respectable capitalist will not do. He will not shoot down his business rival in cold blood, as his savage ancestor would have done to the man who thwarted him in his plans. He will not poison his rival's best workmen nor dynamite his plant in order to cripple his enterprise. Now, if a decent regard for the interests of a competitor in business can be carried thus far, it is plain that it can be carried still farther. It can be enlarged until it will not consent to make profit by exploiting the labor of children; it will not, for its own gain, ruthlessly destroy a weaker man's business; it will not be willing to maintain conditions of labor which involve the inevitable degradation of the laborer. It is simply a question of degree, and those same Scriptures which have shown themselves a store-house of moral energy can be depended upon to equip men for a social *régime* where industry shall be ruled by a more enlightened and more insistent moral sense—a *régime* as far in advance of present-day methods as our own civilization is an improvement upon savagery.

The sublime conception of a redeemed humanity which shall be in the language of the Bible as " one body," with the Divine Christ as its Eternal Head, has never been surpassed. This ideal contemplates a state of society so unified by that sense of intelligent, sympathetic responsibility, which shall perform the function of a nervous system, and so related to Christ, whose mind has become the informing principle of its life, that the injury or the interest of each member shall become the interest of all. If you should venture to prod a lion with a sharp stick anywhere, in the highest and most sensitive or in the lowest, dullest part of him, you would have the whole force of the lion turned upon you instantly in defence of that one of his members which had been made to suffer. And the high task of the minister of religion is to aid in making the whole fabric of society in all its industrial, political, and social relations so truly " one body in Christ " by reason of its thorough permeation with intelligent social interest, that all its members shall have the same care one for another. In that day the strong will gladly bear the infirmities of the weak, and the weak will share joyously in the greater effectiveness of strength. As we strive together for the realization of this eternal purpose, we shall indeed prove what is that good and acceptable and perfect will of God for the organized life of men!

CHAPTER III

In the last lecture I spoke to you regarding the value of a biblical basis for the social message. In order to illustrate this method of using ancient Scripture, and to bring out as well the real content of the book in its bearing on modern social problems, I wish to take up with you now in several lectures the Book of Exodus, dealing with it entirely on the sociological side. This book might not inappropriately be called " The Story of an Ancient Labor Movement "—that title would serve to indicate what is really the main theme of the narrative.

When we pass from the first book in the Bible to the second, we leave behind us the stories of isolated individuals—we take up the history of a race. The Book of Genesis is mainly a series of personal narratives about Adam and Noah, Abraham and Isaac, Jacob and Joseph; it deals with the fortunes and misfortunes of individuals and families considered quite apart from the intricate relationships of a more highly organized life. But when we turn the page and begin the study of Exodus, we find that it enters immediately into the consideration of the relation of God to the industrial and political, to the social and religious well-being of a whole people. The whole scope of the book is therefore broader than that of Genesis, the main interest of the narrative attaching as it does to the working out of certain social problems. Little or nothing is said to Moses, or, indeed, to any one, regarding his individual salvation; there is no hint or promise given to any one of any personal immortality; the message of God throughout is addressed frankly to the needs of the organized life of those early Israelites.

The word " exodus " means literally " the way out." It describes the methods by which a certain people made their way out—out of industrial slavery into industrial freedom; out of a condition which meant the defeat of what is best in life into a condition which made possible happy industry and beautiful home life, made possible the rise of the poet and the prophet, and really paved the way for the rearing of that splendid stock from which should spring the One who, as Son of man, has become the supreme figure in human history. " The way out," then, the freeing and training, the humanizing and spiritualizing of a whole race of men, who at the beginning of the story were the slaves of Pharaoh—

this is the splendid theme of the Book of Exodus. Any one can see instantly how rich such a book may be in suggestive symbolism for the whole movement toward social and industrial betterment in our own time.

It is profoundly significant that this second book in the Bible does have for its main theme, not individual safety and culture so much as the regeneration of an entire people through a radical modification of the industrial and political conditions under which they lived. The compiler of the narrative does not forget the importance of making the inner purpose right, but he is also profoundly interested in the bearing of environment upon character, and he is particularly insistent upon just and equitable relations between man and man. It has often been remarked that the first question asked in the Bible is, " Adam, where art thou? " And the second question is like unto it, the other half of it, " Cain, where is thy brother? " Thus the great God who walked in the garden in the cool of the day, when the shadows of evening and of guilt were falling together across the pathway of His erring children, made His searching inquiries touching the two fundamental attitudes of men. " Where art thou " in thine own attitude toward God, and " Where is thy brother " as a result of the way you have borne yourself toward him—on these two fundamental inquiries hang all the law and the prophets!

I shall try, then, in several of the lectures which are to follow, to tell briefly the story of this ancient labor movement as recorded in the Book of Exodus, and so to interpret it as to show its bearing upon modern conditions. I shall also seek to indicate the contribution it makes to that social appeal which the modern pulpit is to embody in its total message to our own times. And in the consideration of the essential teaching of this book I wish to notice first " the oppression of an entire people."

" There arose up a new king over Egypt, who knew not Joseph." This king was a practical, hard-headed man of affairs. He was not to be swerved from his course by any unprofitable sentiment. "Come, now," he said, " let us deal wisely with them, lest they multiply and fight against us." Therefore Pharaoh " did set over them taskmasters to afflict them with burdens. And the Egyptians made the children of Israel to serve with rigor, and they made their lives bitter with hard bondage."

In all probability we can walk about as far back into ancient history with sure tread and solid certainty in the land of Egypt as in any other land upon the globe. Dean Stanley, in his well-known " History of the Jewish Church," discusses this point at considerable length. " The land of Egypt is to this hour rich in monuments and exhibits of its ancient life. The clear, dry climate, the nearness of the desert sands which have preserved what they overwhelmed, the passionate desire of the old Egyptians to perpetuate every familiar and loved object as long as human power and skill could compass it, have all contributed to this result."

The preserving and embalming customs of that ancient people were such that we can go back and look upon their household utensils and wall decorations, their toys and their games, their articles of personal adornment and their books. We can even go back and look upon the very forms and faces of those men and women who lived and died forty centuries ago. Some years ago when I stood in the great Gizeh Museum at Cairo looking upon the mummied face and form which is pronounced by eminent archæologists to be undoubtedly that of Ramses II, the Pharaoh of the oppression, it was all so intensely lifelike that I could almost see the wizened face frowning in angry refusal, and hear the dry lips breaking their long silence to say: " Who is the Lord, that I should obey his voice and let Israel go! "

The references to the presence of the Hebrews in Egypt in the inscriptions of that country are so scanty and uncertain as to make impossible any valuable corroboration of the biblical narrative from this source. But after a careful sifting of all the evidence the net result seems to be about this: that there was a sojourn in Egypt of uncertain duration; that it was a time of suffering and deprivation; and that the fact of a providential deliverance became the great political and religious background for the whole movement of growth and progress among the Hebrew people.

The references in Exodus to the scenes and customs of the country are so far in keeping with what we know of ancient Egypt from other sources, and the impress of Egypt upon the later thought and life of Israel is so apparent, that we have abundant and reliable materials for study in these narratives of Exodus, even though they may have been expanded, retouched, and edited by later hands in the interests of theological theory. The great fact of an oppression is there, and our intimate knowledge of what conscript or slave labor meant in those ancient monarchies, intent upon huge building operations for the creation of such treasure cities as Pithom and Ramses, or in the erection of such regal tombs as the Pyramids, or in laying together the mighty walls of their cities, enables us readily to picture to ourselves the condition of these children of Israel in the days when " the Egyptians caused them to serve with rigor and made their lives bitter with hard bondage."

The power of the monarch was absolute; his actual wealth may have been less than that of some modern capitalist, but his power over the bodies and minds, over the lives and destinies of hundreds and thousands of dependent people, through his control of the terms and conditions of their existence, was simply absolute. Human life was cheap and abundant. The great building operations, which are the wonder of the world to this hour, were being vigorously carried forward for the gratification of royal pride; and, as a result, the grinding oppression of the helpless poor was simply inevitable. There was on their part, too, such a lack of intelligence and organization, such a lack of ambition and energy sufficient to remedy their status, that they sank down defeated before that which they felt was too great and too hard to be changed.

A recent lecturer in the Lowell Institute at Boston, fresh from his studies of the situation along the Nile, has thus embodied his view of ancient labor conditions in these few terse sentences: "Here in Egypt are the tombs of kings, stupendous monuments not alone of monarchical glory and pride, but of the reckless waste of innumerable human lives. Deep in the sands dug a myriad of slaves, ignorant of everything save the stern necessity of yielding up every bit of strength in their bodies, and every last gleam of intelligence in their minds, to the demands of the king. In the quarries, on the roads, and on the walls for scores of years there toiled these thousands of men, wageless and half-fed, overworked and scourged, sick, dizzy, and exhausted. The only hospital they knew was the taskmaster's whip, which stimulated into one last, agonized effort the exhausted muscles of a used-up body or the frenzied movement of a reeling brain. Whether the glory of the monarch demanded the speedy completion of some expression of his selfish pride, or a too rapidly growing race must be reduced to manageable proportions without massacre, the whole picture of that useless, grinding toil testifies to an ugly, wicked contempt for human life."

Do you wonder, then, that the author of the Scripture narrative, seeing it all, knowing how the Egyptians forced the children of Israel to " serve with rigor and made their lives bitter with hard bondage," came to believe that the sight of it touched the heart of God in heaven and brought from Him, as we shall see later, that mighty intervention on their behalf?

And, alas! has it all gone? Would that all this were only a painful chapter of far-away history. But you can strike out the words " Egypt " and " Israel," if you will, and read the sentences I have just quoted as an accurate description of many situations in the life of our own Republic. Here in our own world of modern industry the prosperous and the fortunate have forced many of the children of America to serve with rigor, and have made their lives bitter with hard bondage. It is not the frightful slavery of ancient Egypt, or of Rome, or of our own Southern States a generation ago, but we have all about us other conditions which jar almost as harshly upon the modern conscience, made sensitive as it is by increased attention to the social ideals of Jesus Christ.

Are there not wage-slaves among us—the main difference being that their virtual owners have now been freed from the responsibility of caring for them when they are sick or unemployed? Are there not hundreds of weary working-men, taxed steadily beyond their strength, wearing out before their time, receiving far less than an equitable share of the prosperity they help to create, and forced by necessity to serve with rigor? Are there not hundreds of tired clerks and book-keepers, insufficiently paid, working often far into the night, in close, dark quarters, with abundance of bad air, sometimes in those hideous little " upper berths " of offices put in against the ceiling like swallows' nests to save floor space and rent? And all the while many of those who reap the profit from this exacting labor are rejoicing in a useless and debilitating luxury which is made possible for them by the lack of equity in the sharing of the profits of the business. Have not New York and Chicago and San Francisco something to say about lives made bitter with hard bondage, as well as Thebes and Karnak? Are there not thousands of breaker boys at the mines in Pennsylvania, and of bobbin girls in the cotton-mills of the South, and of factory hands, both men and women, in all the huge manufactories, whose physical health and mental unfolding, whose spirit of hope and moral stamina are being ruthlessly undermined by the grinding demand for large profits and good dividends, in order to swell still further the most extravagant scale of living, on the part of great numbers of the prosperous members of society, which this world has ever witnessed? Serving with vigor, embittered by hard bondage, driven by the imperative tale of bricks, until their hearts fail within them and many of the toilers lapse into a dull, sodden state, which is an ugly caricature of what human existence was meant to be—is not all this modern experience as well as ancient history?

I am not thinking now of the intemperate denunciations uttered by some noisy street-corner agitator, though more often than not he may be telling that part of the truth which he sees and feels. Take the carefully considered words of competent and reliable men who have patiently investigated the situation. Read Charles Booth's scientifically accurate and painstaking volumes on " The Life and Labor of the People of London." Read the chapters of " America's Working Class," by the late Charles B. Spahr, of the *Outlook*, who was sent out by that paper to observe the conditions of the working-people in New England and Pennsylvania, in the Southern States, and in the Middle West. Read " The Present South," by Edgar Gardner Murphy, himself a Southern man, born, educated, and reared in the South, and from personal observation bearing this testimony: " I have seen and photographed children of six and seven at labor in our factories for twelve and thirteen hours a day. I have seen them with their little fingers mangled by machinery and their little bodies limp and listless with exhaustion. And I am not willing that our economic progress should be involved with such conditions, or that our important and distinctive industry should stand in such moral and economic odium." Read Dr. Peter Roberts's book " The Anthracite Coal Communities," which brings before us a sorry picture of the physical, mental, and moral deterioration which is going on in the State of Pennsylvania by the employment of the immature in and about the coal mines. Read

the sombre chapters of Robert Hunter's book on
"Poverty," the materials for which he gathered to
a considerable extent with his own hands. Read the
records of the actual facts which honest men and
women have seen with their eyes, and handled with
their hands, and felt in their own quivering flesh,
as they have shared the toil of struggling thousands
in America to-day, and if you are not made of stone
you will again hear the cry, "Forced to serve with
rigor; lives embittered with hard bondage!" And
in the face of this lack of any real opportunity to
maintain health and hope, to work with joy and
courage, to grow intellectually or to gain spiritual
peace, you will listen closely to ascertain if the
heavens do not again open and a divine voice cry
out once more: "Let my people go, that they may
serve me." The oppression of great numbers of people, because they are helpless under the wheels of
a huge system, has not ceased, and it still must settle
its accounts with the One whose sympathies went
out to those struggling Israelites on the banks of the
Nile, and there became effective for their relief.

The reasons for this ancient oppression are made
plain by the narrator. First, there was a demand
for cheap labor in order to maintain the luxurious
life of Pharaoh and his nobles—a social principle
which has been in constant operation from that day

to this. The total productive power of the race naturally increases as machinery and new inventions open the way, but it is always definite and limited. It is easily possible, however, under an equitable system of distribution that the entire right-minded, industrious portion of the race should, with this total product of their toil, be comfortable and happy. But where one family insists on spending a hundred thousand dollars a year for its sustenance and pleasure, it means that there must be curtailment somewhere else, even to the point of want and bitterness, for it would be impossible to show that this single family has by its own exertions contributed in anything like that ratio to the actual production of wealth—it is to a considerable extent exploiting the productive labor of others. If, then, we are to have an unreasonable and unjust extreme of luxury at one end of the scale, we must have an unreasonable and unjust extreme of penury at the other end. The heartless luxury and the consequent demand for cheap labor in Egypt thus aided in reducing the Israelites to the sorry condition in which we find them at the opening of the book.

There was also, we are told, the frankly expressed desire to reduce a too rapidly growing class to manageable proportions. If the patient beasts of burden in human society had taken it into their heads to change the *régime* which saddled them with burdens grievous to be borne, it might have been embarrassing to those who were only too willing to profit by their oppression. Pharaoh and his nobles had a vague fear of those sturdy Hebrews, who were then, as now, a vital, productive race. He therefore decided to make the conditions of their employment such as to reduce their physical vitality, thus reducing their numbers and lessening the menace they might offer upon occasion to the system which supported him.

But more fundamental than all else was the fact that their well-being had depended solely upon personal favor. Joseph, the first Hebrew to settle in Egypt, had been a favorite of Pharaoh, and while he lived all the Hebrews shared in that good fortune. " But Joseph died, and all that generation, and a new king arose, who knew not Joseph." Then, because their well-being depended on personal favor, their lot was suddenly changed, and they found themselves ground under the rigor imposed by the Pharaoh of the oppression.

Favor on personal grounds is common in all Oriental countries, and is not uncommon in other lands, as may be seen in the bestowal of political patronage where civil-service rules have not been applied, or in unregulated industry where a bad night's sleep or a fit of indigestion on the part of some superintendent may cost a wage-earner his job; and everywhere such a situation is full of danger. With human nature as it now is some more effective system for securing justice to all concerned, some court of appeal or fair-minded tribunal, where both parties have a hearing, is surely demanded. The interests of the working-people are never sufficiently safeguarded where employment, the chance of a livelihood, and the possibility of advancement are habitually given or withheld on grounds of personal favor, as is the case in unorganized and unregulated industry.

The effects of this oppression went much deeper than the mere physical suffering involved. It is sad enough to see people working from hard necessity under such conditions that their food is cheap in quality and insufficient in quantity; their clothing hardly sufficing for decency, and adding little or nothing of comfort and beauty; their homes unfit to be the growing places for little children, made in the image of God but rapidly losing the divine imprint. All this—the insufficiency of food, raiment, shelter—is sad enough, but sadder still is the fact that the human spirit, under such conditions, loses its spring and zest, its aspiration and hope. It becomes dull, sodden, low; it grows craven, cowardly, abject under its hard lot; it comes to have the gait and bearing of the slave, rather than that of the free man. The hopeless degradation of that manhood, which is meant to shine as the summit and glory of creation, the highest expression of Infinite Power and Wisdom—this is the terrible fact about industrial oppression!

When that representative of the *Outlook,* Mr. Charles B. Spahr, went through some of the cotton-mills of New England he found there, working with the men and women, hundreds of children, some of them as young as thirteen, though that was against the published rules; but to his surprise he saw no men apparently older than forty or forty-five. He remarked upon this fact, for the mills had been in operation many years, and there would naturally have been a percentage of older operatives in these factories. He was promptly told that the strain was so severe that men were worn out at forty-five, and being no longer able to keep the pace they were ruthlessly thrown aside. They then either had to seek other employment, which was hard to obtain for men of forty-five who knew nothing but the cotton-mill, or else fall back upon their families. In the latter event one of two things happened—either the wife, usually a trifle younger than her husband and with nimbler feminine fingers, took his place in the factory, while the husband began to do the housework and tend the children; or else his children, who were old enough to stand at the spinners and the looms, went into the factory to support him by their untimely labor, when they ought to have been playing or at school. An idle father, whether his idleness be enforced or voluntary, and a wage-earning child are always symptoms of an abnormal and degraded industrial condition.

Picture it to yourselves! The demand for cheap goods so imperative, the insistence upon profits for the manufacturers so peremptory, the pace of industry consequently so sharp, that men are frequently thrown aside at forty-five! They are thus doomed to a premature old age, in which, though the outward man perish, the inward man is not renewed day by day. A well-known superintendent in the steel industry when questioned on this point recently bore similar testimony by saying frankly and bluntly: " It is all true. The way we have to rush things now makes it necessary for us to get in a batch of men, work them out, and then get a fresh batch." At the very time when their manhood ought to be in its glory, the men in those cotton factories found themselves worn out, thrown aside for nimbler-fingered women and children, and compelled sorrowfully to take up the tasks of cooking and washing, of sweeping and mending, of bringing to the factory, with shame and mortification written all over them, the lunch for the wife and children, who had now become the real bread-winners of the family!

The children themselves, meanwhile, taken from the school-rooms, where they might be studying, and from the open air, where they might be playing, are sent to breathe cotton-waste and factory dust, to inhale the odor of machine oil, and to labor long and weary hours amid the din and roar of clanking looms! What type of human being will such a process ultimately produce? Devouring greed is here making itself the enemy of the entire race by crushing the tiny seeds of its future life! Such a system saps the toilers of all joy and zest, of all hope and cheer of the higher sort; it leaves them a lot of human machines finding their relief and relaxation mainly in the grosser indulgences of the flesh, for so long as work is made unnatural, pleasures will be unnatural too; and it keeps them hopeless, for they know that erelong they, too, will be cast aside before their time to make room for a fresher lot!

And all this in a world made by Him whose tender mercies are over all His works, who intends that every little child shall in its innocent unfolding be like a sample and foretaste of the kingdom of heaven! The spiritual tragedy of it all stands out naked and ugly. To kill a child quickly with poison is a crime;

and to kill a child slowly, by destroying all possibility of the higher physical, mental, and spiritual effectiveness, through the greed of some employer, is also a crime, whether the statute-books say so or not. The farmer has sense enough and conscience enough not to put the burden of sustained labor on his immature colts and calves. Shall our industrial life care more for the beasts of the field than it does for these little ones for whom Christ died?

This oppression of the children of Israel aided in knitting them together into a mutually reliant and indestructible brotherhood. There is no fellowship in the world like the fellowship of suffering. Burdens borne together bring a solidarity of feeling thicker than the kinship of blood. Members of the Grand Army of the Republic stand together to-day, strong-knit in their fraternal feeling because they have marched and fought, they have hungered and suffered together in a common cause. The cross of Christ has become the leading symbol in the world's moral history and the rallying point of its holiest endeavor, because there He suffered for men; and because there also we catch the sacrificial spirit which prompts us to stand beside Him in the great task of redeeming the world from wrong. These Hebrews, by their experience of a common oppression, likewise received a baptism of suffering which bound the

hearts of that race into a wondrous unity which en-
dures to this hour, though for twenty centuries they
have been men without a country. By burdens borne
together there was begotten a class sympathy, a loyal
unity, and a race consciousness which would have
value for the betterment of the whole group. The
narrow individual interests and rivalries began to
seem petty in the presence of the fraternal spirit
which prompted this vaster undertaking for the
common good, in the face of this broader movement
for national well-being. Progress was being made
toward the day when the common consciousness would
be, ' We are all members one of another, and if one
member suffer all the members suffer with it.'

This sore oppression was not endured without remonstrance from the toiling people. When the tale
of bricks was doubled the people cried to Pharaoh:
" Wherefore dealest thou thus with thy servants? "
Nor was the protest voiced alone in human resentment; the word of the Lord rang out to Pharaoh,
saying, "Let my people go, that they may serve me!"
This divine summons was more fundamental than a
mere demand that the people receive a more equitable share of the results of their toil in food, clothing,
and other material advantages. It was God's word
of searching rebuke to industrial conditions unjust
and degrading; it was His appeal to the powerful and

prosperous class which was responsible for those conditions to change them; and it was also the proclamation of His interest in and His purpose for each
humble toiler. " Let my people go, that they may
serve me "—that they may live human lives, that
they may have homes worthy of the name, that they
may enjoy the social and intellectual, the civil and
spiritual privileges which belong to normal existence!
All this was implied in that divine remonstrance.

In fact the very heart of the whole industrial question is contained in that brief sentence which burst
from the skies and fell upon the astonished ears of
Pharaoh, the oppressor. The divine sympathy is
there—" My people! " Not a horde of nameless
slaves, the property of an irresponsible monarch; not
so many thousand " hands " herded together by some
careless factory owner; not " the wage-earning class "
of some chilly economist, but—" My people! " The
divine purpose for all these toilers is there—" that
they may serve me." It lies within the gracious purpose of God that every life born into the world should
grow tall and straight, sound and clean, by the consecration of its powers to His service. And the divine demand for adequate opportunity is also there
—" Let my people go," for these struggling souls
must be released from terms so hard as to utterly
defeat the divine purpose for their spiritual unfold-

ing. In all the earnest appeals of poet and prophet, of essayist and reformer, in modern times, I find no message to social conditions which bears upon its face more clearly the divine credential than that same word of the Lord to Pharaoh, " Let my people go, that they may serve me ! "

And how did that monarch and the ruling classes generally receive this divine remonstrance ? Did they recognize their common humanity with all the struggling millions who do the rough work of the world ? Did they feel an instant throb of sympathy for those hard-pressed people, with brains under their hats, thinking, wondering, wishing, despairing; with hearts in their breasts filled with hopes and fears, with loves and hates ? Did there come to them any sense of common allegiance to Him who is no re-specter of persons or of classes or of outward condi-tions, but who is intent, ever and only, on the pur-pose and disposition of the life within ? Did any sense of responsibility to the One Father, who has created us all, impel them to deal fairly and humane-ly with those toiling people whose lot and destiny were at their mercy ? You know the answer which came back to this divine remonstrance—an indiffer-ent, heartless, insolent refusal; it was: " Who is the Lord, that I should obey his voice to let Israel go ? "

There was in that city on the Nile an unjust judge, who neither feared God nor regarded man. He refused, so long as his own life was pleasant and happy, to concern himself about the lot of those toilers on whose patient, bleeding shoulders rested the great industrial structure whose advantages he monopolized. And when the wickedness of it was laid before him in that divine protest, the insolent reply was: " Who is the Lord, that I should obey his voice to let Israel go ? "

The inhumanity of it sounds a thoroughly brutal note. Is it right, between man and man, that one class of people should live as slaves, their bodies, brains, and spirits bought and sold, used and abused by the whim of any master who has money enough to own them, in order that another class of people may live in ease and luxury ? Is that right ? This was the question God asked Pharaoh in Egypt, and He has been asking it all down the centuries since. It has taken the race a long time to answer it. It was not answered in our own country until thousands of men went down to Shiloh and Vicksburg, to Antietam and Gettysburg, to answer God's solemn question, " Is it right ? " And there amid the roar of cannon and the rattle of musketry, the answer went up that it was not right—the social conditions of human slavery were wrong and were therefore banished once for all from this land of freedom!

But is it right to-day that one man should give his whole life and the lives of his children, as soon as they are old enough to leave school and work, for a bare subsistence—for a tenth or a twentieth, it may be, of what is recklessly wasted in the home of his employer? Is it right that one mortal should live in a useless and debilitating luxury, able to satisfy every trifling fancy, while many of those whose labor he has exploited, every whit his equals, it may be, in original moral endowment, should be unable to secure the bare necessities? Is that type of distribution right? The same great God who discussed economic questions with Pharaoh on the banks of the Nile thirty odd centuries ago is still pressing home upon the consciences of people to-day that same vital question. And He will continue to press it home until it, too, is answered, and answered right!

May it be that all ears shall be attentive to His call and all hearts responsive to the approach of His Spirit, so that this question may not be answered on the field of battle, or in terms of blood, or in any violent overthrow of the institutions of society, but answered, rather, in the peace and quiet of better industrial methods, gradually and steadily introduced, in the reign of a more complete justice between man and man, in the prevalence of a more considerate spirit infused into all those activities which yield us bread! The question will never be withdrawn, we may be sure, until men have the courage and the conscience to answer it right. Cruelty, inhumanity, injustice, when they become plain, as modern literature and current economic discussion are making them plain to us, must be remedied and corrected, or there will inevitably fall upon us, too, the sore plagues of God's rebuke. Pharaohs are being bred to-day in modern counting-rooms as they were in the palaces along the Nile; and, like their ancient predecessors, many of them are heedless of the voice of the Spirit, as He speaks through the cry of the plain people whose patient labor makes possible their showy prosperity.

It is as dangerous to-day as it was under the oppression in Egypt for any man, or for any set of men, or for any system, to stand up and say, " Who is the Lord that we should let these people go into a larger, finer life? " It is a selfish, heartless course, and one certain to bring disaster. Those lines of action which spring naturally from unmodified self-interest bring in, not the kingdom of heaven, but the kingdom of hell. They have in recent years been bringing in great sections of it in our own land.

This same old note of inhumanity is heard ever

and anon in our modern life. Sometimes it falls
from the lips of the prosperous indifferent; sometimes it is written in an unjust wage-scale; sometimes it is embodied in a whole system of production which means cruelty to the helpless. You will
find instructive testimony on this point in the writings of John Graham Brooks, for example, one of
the careful, conservative observers of labor conditions, never an agitator, yet so deeply interested in
modern problems that he has taken pains to visit
the scene of every important coal strike for the
last eighteen years. He recently made a study also
of the conditions prevailing in the Southern cotton-
mills, and he has given us an account of this investigation. We have also the testimony of many other
competent witnesses regarding the same matter, and
the plain facts are appalling to our sense of justice
and humanity! Troops of children, many of them
under twelve years of age, are dragged out of their
little beds to have their meagre breakfasts hurried
down their throats, and are rushed off to the mill
with sleepy eyes, to toil amid the roar of machinery
for eleven hours a day. Their homes are often narrow, dirty, ill-smelling sties, on the edge of a marsh,
with fever and malaria stalking across the threshold
bringing death in their train. The pinched and
broken little waifs look up sad-eyed and wistful,

making their mute appeal for a human existence. And when the owners and managers of the mills were asked why they used child-labor, they replied, "We have to do it! We have to do it to compete with other mills and keep up our profits." Last year sixty per cent of the operatives in the spinning departments of the cotton-mills of the South were under sixteen years of age. In North Carolina sixteen per cent of them were under fourteen, and at the opening of the year there were in all the Southern cotton-mills twenty thousand children under twelve years of age.

And on those ill-gotten profits the owners and managers of the mills were living, not on the edge of the marsh in narrow, filthy quarters, but yonder, on the hills, in beauty and luxury; trading on the blood and tears of children under twelve, who had been thrust forward by parents willing to have them there because their own wages were too small adequately to support the family! Is that right? "We have to do it," they said, "to keep our profits up!" Who is the Lord, that we should let these children go, and be compelled to scale down our own luxurious existence? The essential note of the two replies, that of old Pharaoh and that of such a modern mill-owner, is the same—it is the note of selfish, insolent inhumanity!

It is said, in attempted extenuation of this practice, that these children had been accustomed to
work on the farms from which they came. But
it is one thing to work out of doors, at varied tasks,
with the intermissions of rainy seasons and periods
of leisure common to country life, with the companionship of living things and under the eye of a
father; it is quite another thing to engage in the
stolid and unbroken labor of a factory. As one man,
who had witnessed both, has well said: " Letting
your own children work for you is a very different
thing from letting another man work your children."
A divine law is grossly violated when young girls
of twelve and fourteen and sixteen are compelled
to stand all day working month in and month out
without interruption—a divine law is violated which
the State of Alabama did not enact, and which it
cannot repeal. And in view of the fact that the
future vigor of that portion of the human race is
there being determined, society cannot afford to look
with indifference upon this poisoning of the stream
of human life at its source.

You will find the same spirit of inhumanity also
in the North, for selfishness knows no Mason and
Dixon's line. In the fall of 1902, as winter came
on, we were fast in the grip of the great coal strike.
It had been on for months. Cellars were empty.

The bins of the coal dealers held but a meagre supply. The demand for coal was great; the price was forced up, and the poor people of New York, Chicago, and other large cities found themselves unable to buy coal at all. They were doing their bit of cooking on little oil-stoves. Some of them, in dark, chilly rooms, were burning these stoves day and night to protect their shivering children from the cold. Everywhere among the poor the little coal-oil stove was pressed into service because it was cheaper than coal.

Then just at that juncture the men who control that mighty organization known as the Standard Oil Company caused the price of coal-oil to be advanced. There was not even the pretence of a claim that this was necessary because of an increase in the cost of producing the oil. The market was keen; the people, especially the poor, had to have it, because coal was not to be had, and there was a clear chance to add several extra millions to the annual profits of the Standard Oil Company; and so the price was advanced. You will recall the angry protest which instantly went up all over the land from secular and religious papers alike, but the higher price remained, and the children of the poor were thrust that much closer to the peril of unheated rooms and of uncooked food! Indifference, inhumanity, cruelty to the helpless—alas, they are not ancient history, for the advance in the price of coal-oil was but a modern echo of Pharaoh's words, ' Who is the Lord, that I should obey his voice and let these people go ? '

We are informed by those who have utilized the statistics carefully gathered by men and women who are working in the East End of London in connection with the University and Social Settlements, that there are at least eight hundred thousand people there who are habitually underfed. These unfortunates never know from year's end to year's end the joy and strength of three full meals in one day. Because of this they are losing health and ambition; they are losing intelligence and effectiveness; they are dropping down into the abyss. And meanwhile, there are, also, more than a hundred thousand able-bodied men in England who put themselves down in the census as of " No occupation." They work at nothing; they are living, many of them, on hereditary estates, dwelling in noble city palaces and in lovely country seats surrounded by acres and acres of park and game preserve, taking their lordly pleasure, while thousands of their fellow-Englishmen are starving—starving when they might be living by the cultivation of that very land held as game preserve for the amusement of many useless idlers! Picture

to yourselves the cold-blooded, insolent inhumanity
of it! Sumptuous idleness standing over against the
actual starvation of ill-requited toil!

I talked once with a gentleman who stood on the
streets of Manchester, England, peeling an orange,
and when he flung away the peel it was instantly
seized upon by hungry children and greedily eaten
before his eyes. Earlier in the day he had stood at
the entrance of one of the great mills and had seen
the mothers of some of these same children hand
in their infants at the door of a *crèche* to pass into
the mill to work for ten hours, receiving their infants back at the close of the day to carry them away
to such wretched homes as factory wages enabled
them to maintain. What sort of people would that
type of housekeeping eventually produce? And what
sort of character was growing in the lives of their
employers who were living on the profits of that
system in palaces which he also visited, palaces which
would have been appropriate for the kings and
queens of an earlier generation?

With his contemptuous refusal of justice to the
helpless Israelites Pharaoh also coupled this further
heartless statement: " Ye are idle; ye are idle." It
was quite in the vein of that modern reproach uttered now and then to the unfortunate poor: " You
don't work. You don't want to work. You are not

thrifty; it is your own fault that you do not succeed."

We have all heard at one time or another such unsympathetic words from the lips of prosperous selfishness; and we have heard men say that any industrious man who really wants work can always get it. It is a statement which in vast numbers of cases goes wide of the mark. As pastor of a large city church I have more personal friends among the employers of labor than has the average wage-earner—a great many more—and any one of them would count it a pleasure to do me a favor. Yet with all this, I have often tramped about for half a day at a time to get employment for some man out of work, and have come back in the evening as heavy-hearted as he was, to tell him I had failed. The door to employment does not stand forever open, nor does it always swing easily on its hinges at the touch of willing industry. " Modern life has no more tragic figure than the gaunt, hungry laborer wandering about the great centres of industry and wealth, begging for permission to share in that industry and to contribute to that wealth, asking in return not the luxuries or even the comforts of civilized life, but only such rough food and shelter for himself and family as would be practically assured to him in the rudest form of savage society." To reproach all the unemployed with the charge of laziness and unwillingness to work is often nothing better than inhuman insolence. The working-people have their faults, for they are human beings like the rest of us, but the marvel is, that handicapped as so many of them often are, they make such a brave attempt at honest, self-supporting, self-respecting lives.

The inhumanity in modern life does not spring so much from any personal hard-heartedness as from the peremptory demands of a system. Man to man, there never was so much genuine kindness on earth as there is right now. It is never difficult to get money to relieve a case of actual suffering—the difficulty is in securing that intelligent and persistent attention to those better industrial methods which will obviate a large percentage of the poverty and distress. Those men who are striving to conduct their business enterprises in the spirit of Christian humanity—and there are many of them—are constantly hindered in their more generous purposes by the ruthless competition of those to whom " business is business," while conscience and the higher laws of right are quite another matter. Back of the manufacturer, who feels compelled to fill his factory with the cheap labor of women and children, is the wholesaler urging him to sell his goods cheap or he will buy elsewhere. And back of the wholesaler is the retailer, and " back of them all, the careless, bargain-hunting public, throwing its whole weight into the effort to keep prices down." And yonder, where all these cheap things are produced, life grows cheap, and the shocking inhumanity of the system becomes a reproach to our modern civilization.

It is the clear duty of every one who has awakened to his social responsibility to set himself against the whole spirit of such a system. The useful service rendered by the Consumers' League, which has done so much to make the buying public conscious of the moral issues involved in the exercise of its purchasing power and to organize it in such a way as to make its influence felt in the discouragement of unwholesome methods of production, is a significant and hopeful symptom in our modern life. We do not want to wear shirts, for example, from the bargain counter, no matter how cheaply we can buy them, if the cotton was spun by children who ought to have been studying at school or playing in the open air; if the shirts themselves were made by tired factory girls, huddled together in close quarters, and working long hours at a dying wage; if the shirts are sold over counters by girls in a department-store, kept on such a close margin of wages as to make the temptation to a life of shame stand before them as a constant and alluring alternative. We cannot consent to clothe ourselves, however small may be the expense of it, upon the blood and tears of those who have been robbed and harmed by the effort to produce the clothing cheap. We cannot become partners in Pharaoh's inhumanity and say: "Who are all these unknown workers, that we should care for them?"

This sense of social responsibility is certainly on the increase, and it is becoming a factor which must be increasingly reckoned with even by the high and dry economists who profess themselves to be "untouched by sentiment" in their scientific study of "the reign of economic law." In the words of Owen R. Lovejoy, "We are beginning to learn that nothing is produced for our convenience and comfort without sacrifice somewhere in the process. Society is rising from the plane in which a cash payment for goods was regarded as the final discharge of obligation, and is coming to recognize that we have not discharged all our duty or made full payment for the goods until we have done our utmost to secure to every person engaged in their preparation a fair reward for service, a full share of liberty, and an adequate opportunity for the complete development of body and mind to a symmetrical maturity. That the individual can fulfil this social obligation alone is not expected, but that society must discover methods by which we can be fed and clothed and warmed without oppression or injustice, is fundamental to democracy."

But there was, furthermore, an element of actual blasphemy in Pharaoh's scornful reply to the divine remonstrance. The haughty monarch bade defiance to the whole system of moral and spiritual values, which was being outraged by his course of action. He hurled his contempt at the One who bends His omnipotent energy to the production of higher types of men and women. He spurned the divine capacity in man—the presence of Immanuel, God with us, working within men for their redemption— when he thus uttered his insulting refusal. The very discontent which fired the hearts of those Israelites with the hope of something better was from God. "Blessed are they that hunger"—hunger after righteousness or hunger after anything which means a more abundant life—the hunger itself is evidence of the pressure of the divine Spirit from within: it shows the real capacity of the man rising into self-consciousness. When Pharaoh uttered his contemptuous refusal to this divinely produced discontent in the hearts of the oppressed, which was impelling them to seek a finer, fuller life, it was, therefore, akin to blasphemy.

"Who is the Lord?" he said: "I know not the

Lord!" His blunt statement was fearfully accurate. Pharaoh was unacquainted with the Lord, who speaks through that prophetic discontent which arrays itself against wrong industrial methods, who speaks in the terms of social unrest among the toiling people, who speaks in the very look of the wistful lives foredoomed to failure by the conditions of their existence. "Who is the Lord? I know not the Lord," and by that haughty confession the monarch was already predicting his speedy downfall. If you listen closely you can almost hear the approach of those waves of divine judgment which were to sweep over Pharaoh and his host, swallowing up horse and rider in complete disaster, because of his guilty injustice.

The mind at this point naturally runs ahead to that great judgment scene portrayed by Christ. Jesus pictured Himself as sitting upon His throne, saying to the multitude on His left hand: "I was an hungered and ye gave me no meat; naked and ye clothed me not; sick and in prison and ye visited me not. I was a stranger and ye took me not in." And then in almost indignant surprise, they cried: "Lord, when saw we thee an hungered . . . or naked, or sick or a stranger or in prison and ministered not unto Thee?" They, too, knew not the Lord—they knew not the Lord, who had appeared to them and appealed

to them in the common want, in the oft-recurring
necessities of the plain people. And Jesus answered
them, " Inasmuch as ye did it not to one of the least
of these, ye did it not to me." " Depart from me;
I never knew you."

"I know not the Lord," said Pharaoh of old.
" We knew not the Lord," said the selfish multitude
standing condemned in the day of judgment because
they had not heard the call of Christ in the needs
of the many. And the heartless people of our own
day who fail to discern in the wistful faces of the
helpless poor the beseeching face of the Master
Himself, are, by their course of action, standing in
the same perilous attitude. Inevitably in the hour
of judgment there must come back to them that same
solemn word of condemnation: " Depart from me;
I never knew you."

When any man in the pleasant prosperity of his
own life reaches the point where he can look out
upon the want and pain of the world, upon the failure
and degradation of whole classes in society, upon
the blind struggles of the unskilled, unorganized
hewers of wood and drawers of water, upon the
countless multitudes of plain folk defeated in the
better impulses of their natures by conditions too
hard for them—when any man reaches the point
where he can see all this unmoved and not hear

sounding through it a divine protest and a divine appeal, he may know of a certainty that he is in moral peril! If he can witness all this and yet not know the Lord, who is speaking now to the hearts of men through just such appeals, he is already moving swiftly to that place of divine judgment where that Lord of all the earth may say to him, ' I never knew you. Inasmuch as ye labored not to change the lot of these oppressed people ye labored not for me.'

CHAPTER IV

THE CALL OF AN INDUSTRIAL DELIVERER

In the last lecture I sought to bring before you in modern terms a picture of the sore oppression of those ancient Hebrews. The Egyptians had forced the children of Israel to serve with rigor; the unfeeling taskmasters had made their lives bitter with hard bondage, until all the finer features of their humanity were being marred and blurred under that system of cheap slave-labor which held them in its grip. They were becoming dull, unaspiring, despondent cogs in the great wheels of an industrial machine too huge and too hard to be successfully opposed by any resistance which they could offer.

Their sad condition made strong appeal to the humane hearts of all sympathetic observers, and it also touched the heart of God. Indeed, were not this story of an ancient labor movement to be found somewhere upon the pages of Holy Writ, we should be conscious of a serious omission in the biblical portrayal of the divine character. The claim is confidently made that God's tender mercies are over all His works; and thoughtful men would demand visible evidence of it in some clear picture of the divine love planning, moving, leading the way for just such an industrial deliverance as is outlined in this Book of Exodus. And inasmuch as God works habitually through human agents, we come naturally, therefore, at this point in the record, to the call of a deliverer.

The events which led immediately to the call of a leader in this movement for industrial freedom are well known. The monarch of Egypt, alarmed by the too rapidly multiplying race of slaves, and fearing the result of an uprising should an outbreak occur when Egypt might be engaged in foreign war, issued a decree that for a given period all the male children of these Hebrew slaves should be killed at birth. The execution of this fearful edict carried anguish far and wide, for the poor woman suffers when her baby dies exactly as does the rich woman. But the mother of one promising baby boy succeeded in preserving the life of her child by a skilful appeal to the sympathies of Pharaoh's daughter. It was arranged that the princess should find the smiling infant in an ark of bulrushes floating upon the bosom of the sacred Nile. Her womanly sympathies having been thus enlisted, she was induced to give her royal permission to the mother of the babe to keep him and to nurse him under her direction.

In the mind of an Egyptian the Nile was no ordinary river—it was, as Stanley said, " sacred, beneficent, solitary, the very life of the state, the source of all fertility." Many devout Egyptians all but worshipped it. This Nile child, then, " drawn out " of the water, as one of the possible derivations of his name might suggest, at the command of the princess, became the object of royal favor. And when he grew older he was adopted as the son of Pharaoh's daughter, and was brought up at the court of the king.

But, amid all the pleasant advantages of his new surroundings, his heart beat true to his own class. Moses was ever a Hebrew, and his own personal escape from their hard lot did not for one moment stifle his native sympathies. It will be remembered that in his early manhood he once saw an Egyptian taskmaster beating a Hebrew slave. Race loyalty and class feeling, instant sympathy with the oppressed, and that genuinely democratic spirit which ever characterized him, were strong and warm within his breast. He sprang instantly upon the oppressor, and in the hot anger of his resentment actually killed the fellow! The report of this bold act spread rapidly through the city and soon came to the ears of the monarch. Pharaoh knew that a single act of successful violence might start a revolt, and he therefore gave instant command that Moses be slain. Then this warm-hearted champion of the rights of the people was compelled to flee for his life. Out through the desert he went, and on to the quiet land of Midian, in the peninsula of Sinai, seeking safety from the vengeance of the king.

Here, in this quiet retreat in Midian, he was employed by a Kenite sheep-grower named Jethro. Moses kept his master's flocks, and finally, quite in the vein of a modern story, he married one of his employer's daughters. He continued in this simple, pastoral, outdoor life for a series of years, yet never for a moment did he forget the sorrows and afflictions of those Hebrew slaves toiling yonder on the banks of the Nile. But how he, a lone shepherd, could do anything to change their lot or offer any successful resistance to the huge system which lay heavily upon them all, he was unable to see. He felt very much as many an honest man feels to-day when he reads Jacob Riis's " How the Other Half Lives," or London's " People of the Abyss," or John Graham Brooks's " The Social Unrest "—it seems horrible beyond measure, but what can he do about it?

Such a generous impulse, however, once kindled in the breast of a brave man is never forgotten by the God who has all these sacred interests within

His holy keeping.   When Abraham Lincoln was a
young man in Illinois, he went down the river to the
city of New Orleans on business.   While there he
visited a slave-market.   He saw a red-faced, burly
auctioneer selling a comely young mulatto woman,
who stood trembling upon the block.   The girl looked
out into the eyes of a lot of human sharks, who
stood there waiting to bid on her and to buy her,
as she well knew, to her lasting shame.   " Step right
up and examine her, gentlemen, if you wish," bawled
out the auctioneer.   " I never have any secrets from
my customers."   And the strong, pure soul of Lincoln writhed in moral anguish as he saw the ugly
sight.   He looked up to heaven, as he tells us later,
and in silent determination breathed out his vow:
" Great God, if I ever have a chance to hit that
thing, I'll hit it hard! "

Years passed before the chance came, but the Almighty never forgets the splendid vows of uncalculating young souls.   God moved this young man on
in his profession, on through the early struggles in
the political life of his own State, on through his
antislavery speeches in the Douglas debates, on up
to the Wigwam Convention in Chicago, and on to
the White House!   And, finally, the hour struck in
1863; the skies, o'erclouded by dark war, seemed to
clear for a moment, and the Emancipation Procla-

mation shone out. Abraham Lincoln hit it hard, and that Proclamation, sustained and reënforced by the consecrated valor of thousands of brave men, caused the shackles to fall from the legs and arms, from the minds and hearts of four million black folk—kindred, all of them, of that young slave girl whom he had seen on the auction-block in New Orleans! The colored race found a great ally when the heart of the young lawyer was stirred by the new and mighty impulse which came to him in that Crescent City of the South.

And, in similar fashion, the Lord conserved the generous impulse of this young Hebrew, who, in a burst of moral indignation, had killed the Egyptian taskmaster. One day, as Moses led his flock along the slopes of Horeb, he saw a bush burn with a mysterious fire. In those eager, darting flames, ever a symbol of the Divine in the minds of the Semites, he saw the presence of the God he trusted. He heard a divine voice issuing out of the bush. This voice spoke to him not regarding his own personal peace and well-being, it spoke to him of the intolerable conditions under which many of his fellowmen were living, and of his responsibility in the matter. " I am the God thy father, the God of Abraham, and of Isaac, and of Jacob," it said. " I have surely seen the affliction of my people which are in

Egypt and have heard their cry by reason of their taskmasters. I know their sorrows, and I am come down to deliver them." When Moses turned aside to see, the narrator says, " God called unto him out of the midst of the bush." When he became thoughtful and observant of such phenomena as were open to him, even there in the quiet pasture at the foot of Mount Horeb, when he faced the divine approach with interest and sympathy, God spoke to him, and the divine message proved to be a direct call to social service.

It is exceedingly significant that this Moses, the great historic figure in the background of the whole Jewish and Christian movement, the one man to whom the beginnings of a definite moral law in the Bible are referred, was called into the service of God by a direct appeal to his social sympathies. He was called to be the leader in an economic revolution, called to lay the foundations of a commonwealth of free and prosperous industry. ' I have seen the affliction of my people Israel: I have heard their cry by reason of their taskmasters: and I am come down to deliver them; come now, I will send thee unto Pharaoh, that thou mayest bring them out '—these were the terms of the call. And in all the subsequent speeches and writings of Moses we find no word of concern touching his personal salvation, no word regarding his own future destiny or blessed immortality—he was called to lose his life in social service, in order that he might thus find it through the investment of it in the industrial deliverance of his own class.

God turns the scale habitually by the weight of a man. When the tale of bricks is doubled, then Moses comes; and all subsequent history is altered by the strength and wisdom of his splendid leadership. It is at this very point that we seem to find the sorest need in the modern movement toward industrial betterment—there is a grievous lack of worthy leaders. A labor-union man in the city of Baltimore has recently voiced the consciousness of this need in the public prints. " A few years ago I was active in the Federation of Labor, but now, though I am still a delegate, I cannot work in the organization with any enthusiasm. It seems as if working-men are bound to injure themselves by their own actions. They are blindly selfish; they are bitter and short-sighted in their organized procedure. They have no proper, suitable, and intelligent leaders. This is due to the conditions under which they work. They have no chance to educate themselves, or to train leaders from their own ranks. What can you expect in the way of economic discernment from an intelligence which for ten hours a day for six days in the week has been employed in making heads for pins, or upon any other single detail in the modern factory system?"

We can sympathize with this confession of a working-man. His statement that the working-men have "no proper, suitable, and intelligent leaders" seems exaggerated, but there is no sufficient number of such leaders for the heavy task imposed upon the toilers. We have all seen just causes go down in defeat for lack of competent leadership. There are facts enough in the minds of men, feeling enough in the hearts of men, organization enough, class loyalty enough, honest determination enough, but there is, indeed, a sore lack of competent, far-seeing, trustworthy leadership. The hands on the clock of industrial betterment are repeatedly put back, not hours, but days and years, by incompetent leaders, who can feel but not see. Unwise, unjust, violent blows are struck—with honest purpose, it may be, but sure to react to the hurt of the men who struck them. The sympathetic motive must therefore be reënforced and directed by those vast additions of knowledge and experience which come through careful study. Leadership with eyes to see and with ears to hear, with a mind to understand and with real ability to point the way of progress, is the insistent demand of the hour.

The notion that any well-meaning individual who can talk loud and write with red ink ought to be allowed to undertake to upset the existing institutions of society in order to introduce some scheme of his own, does not command any serious or useful following these days. We have been favored in the past with brilliant novels, with stirring orations, and with startling sermons dealing with social problems, which have done much more harm than good. And because of the bad effects of all such, the world stands ready to apply to those men who, without careful study of this difficult subject, " undertake to doctor society on the strength of their own happy intuitions and their own love of hearing themselves explode," the same epithet which it applies to those persons who attempt to practise medicine according to that same easy method.

The leadership which will bring deliverance will never be that narrow, one-eyed sort which can see only the evil there is in the present organization of society, with no appreciation for the good ends already attained, and with no true comprehension of the essential method of evolution according to which the universal forces at work in the world about us habitually conserve, as far as may be, existing forms of life and prevalent conditions, utilizing them as available material to be wrought upon for further

advance. If a man sets out in the spirit of that classical pessimist who said, " There is a tide in the affairs
of men which, taken anyway you please, is bad," he
may at this very hour bring himself to the point
where he will feel that instant and violent revolution
is not only justifiable, but inevitable. History, however, is not commonly made while such men wait,
or in deference to their unbalanced suggestions.
To stir up envy wantonly, to arouse ill-founded
prejudice, to make telling but unfair appeals to ignorance, to exaggerate unhappy conditions, and recklessly to charge others with maliciousness and
crime, is not the straightest road to social betterment—it is no road at all. We need reforms, many
and radical, in my judgment, but they will come
very slightly, if at all, through intemperate and bitter denunciation unaccompanied by any wise suggestions for relief; they will come rather by the
patient application of intelligence, conscience, and
experience to problems too vast and too vital to be
solved rapidly or off-hand.

If we are ever to bring together the opposing
parties in this contest for material gain, it must be
on some higher ground than that of self-interest.
The only way that these large issues can be fully
understood and set in the way of a more satisfactory
adjustment is, I believe, in the light of Christian

faith. The narrow, selfish passions of men must be gradually subordinated to those larger principles of social well-being which look toward the day when, by the introduction of a greatly enlarged consciousness, society shall feel all its members—the feet as well as the hands, and the hands as well as the head and the heart; the humble toilers who live by manual labor no less than the brainy captains of industry or the prophets of the spiritual life. This enlarged social consciousness must become so real that when the feet and hands of society are cold and unclad, when they are dirty or diseased, the whole body will be uncomfortable until that condition is changed. It is only a narrow individualism which allows such conditions to endure to-day. And because this task is large and difficult the leadership must be correspondingly competent.

It is the high office of the Christian pulpit to lead the way in the inculcation of these truer principles of social action. If the ministers of Jesus Christ should ever suffer themselves to become merely the liveried servants of a conventional ecclesiasticism; if they should easily content themselves with grinding out regularly such a weekly grist of services and sermons as would hold together a congregation sufficiently responsive in attention and pew-rents to afford them a basis of existence; if they should accept existing institutions and practices as they find them, skilfully adjusting themselves to those conditions for the less heroic task of cultivating here and there a modest plant of private piety—they would then have already abdicated from the high position to which Jesus originally appointed His ministers. He sent them out with the words, " Ye shall sit upon twelve thrones, judging the tribes of Israel." In the work of shaming low ideals, in rebuking courses of action clearly immoral, in leading the forces of righteousness in their advance against the evils of society, and in extending the sceptre of sympathy, of cheer, and of courage to all those deeper aspirations which look toward the coming of a kingdom truly divine, these appointed ministers of Jesus Christ were to do a work nothing less than regal! " Ye shall sit upon thrones," He said to them as they went forth commissioned to serve under His own royal banner. And the modern pulpit will fall short of its legitimate function in the life of the world if it fails to measure up to this high privilege in contributing genuine moral leadership to the work of social reconstruction.

In addition to furnishing his own quota of helpful leadership in the solution of social problems, the minister of to-day may lend his aid to the development of a better type of leader among those who struggle for their own industrial betterment. There are several significant facts to be noted as to the divinely appointed leadership in this ancient labor movement which we are studying. Moses the deliverer belonged originally to the class he was to lead. He was the son of a man who worked yonder in the slave gang; he had been nursed at the breast of a slave mother. All the advantages secured through his adoption by Pharaoh's daughter never changed this fundamental fact nor altered his ultimate loyalty. When he was come to years he refused to be called the son of Pharaoh's daughter, choosing rather to suffer affliction with his own people than to enjoy the pleasures of an iniquitous system for a season. He might at one point in his career have broken away from his humble ancestry and have belonged permanently to the more fortunate class, but in the spirit of unhesitating loyalty he held fast to his own people, and became in time their effective leader.

In similar fashion, the real captains and lieutenants in the struggle for modern industrial freedom must of necessity come up from the ranks. In the discussion of many of the painful problems now before us, the men who do the rough work of the world, and who receive an all too inadequate reward, have the first right to the floor; and it is in the order of progress that they should insist on being heard. The world wonders sometimes why wise professors of economics from the university, or canny millionaires, should not be permitted to tell these wage-earners what to do and how to do it, thus saving them from the awkward blunders they make in learning the way. But the plain people will not and ought not to follow those leaders blindly. It is in the line of historic development that their true leaders shall be bone of their bone and flesh of their flesh. The very fitness for a larger measure of freedom, with all the added responsibilities it will naturally bring, must come through the hard process of gaining that knowledge for themselves.

We shall see great progress along this line, in my judgment, in the next twenty-five years. The employing class is not drawing off the stronger, brainier, more aspiring wage-earners to-day as it did a generation ago. At that period unoccupied land was abundant, and the more resolute spirits were drawn out and away from the crowded centres. The amount of capital needed to go into business for one's self was much smaller than it is to-day, with the huge department-store, the corporation, and the trust, and therefore the ambition to own his own business was a real incentive to effort, carrying many a wage-earner up into the employing class. But to-day, with the great aggregations of capital and industry, such signal success is for the many simply out of the question, and it therefore ceases to be any real incentive. The amount of economic elasticity in our present system is much less than it was fifty years ago. The stronger, abler, and more resolute wage-earners will almost of necessity remain in their own class, and some of them are destined to become Moses-like leaders in the struggle for social betterment. The result will be that the wage-earning class will not be left unorganized and leaderless to the extent that it has been in past years.

We notice further that Moses was not a raw enthusiast, devoid of insight and experience, but a man trained and educated. He was " learned in all the learning of the Egyptians," we are told, thus sharing actively in the benefits of one of the highest civilizations of that period. He had also been for many years a shepherd in the land of Midian, becoming thoroughly familiar with all the ins and outs of the very region through which, in future years, he was to lead the escaping Israelites. He brought to his task, therefore, the ripened experience of a trained and mature man.

It is interesting, and, I believe, significant also, to notice that he was not a ready talker. When first called to be the leader of a labor movement, and of what proved to be an august moral enterprise as well, he begged to be excused on the ground that he was not eloquent in speech. " I am slow of speech," he said, " and of a slow tongue." He urged this point because he felt that this would entirely disqualify him for the service indicated. It would almost seem as if the divine Author of this ancient social effort, in making choice of a suitable leader, foresaw the fact that in the labor movements of the future the glib talkers would frequently come unduly to the front, to the serious detriment of the movements they espoused. The agitators, the talkers, the orators, the spell-binders have again and again wielded a mighty influence which has not always been for the well-being of their admiring and awe-struck hearers. This Moses, then, slow of speech and slow of tongue, who was to move men not so much by burning orations or fiery appeals as by patient, useful, constructive effort, was called to be the central figure in the deliverance of a people.

It is significant, also, that the symbol of power which he should bear with him was his own rod or shepherd's crook which he had borne in the days of useful manual labor in the land of Midian. He went back to Egypt, to hold aloft, in the presence of the people and as a warning to Pharaoh the oppressor, not the sword of violence, not the priestly censer burning with incense, but the plain rod he had used in keeping sheep. . The tool of industry, when duly consecrated, became the symbol of a divine deliverance. It is likewise the belief of many sane people to-day that our own industrial deliverance is to come, not by the torch and musket of any bloody revolution, not by any mysterious censer which will work magical changes in the structure of society, but rather by the use of the common tools of the workaday world, as we find it now, through the gradual introduction of better methods and a nobler spirit.

The great need still is for men constituted as Moses was—for leaders who know something of history, because certain industrial experiments have been sufficiently tried, and there is no need that every generation should try them over again; for leaders who know something of economics, because the rewards of industry cannot be distributed straight along on the basis of feeling and sentiment in defiance of social justice and economic law; for leaders who know something of morals, because the sources of motive and stimulus, the incitements to activity and honesty, to prudence and thrift, cannot be overlooked by any one who is planning the betterment of a people—in a word, for leaders who are acquainted with all the facts and forces which bear upon the entire situation. The call is loud for trained and skilful leaders, competent enough to grasp the problem and to correctly point the way.

It is not too much to say that this demand for leaders brought up from the ranks can in time be adequately met. The public-school system is producing a higher average of intelligence. The State universities, exacting from their students no tuition fees, or only nominal ones, are making possible the higher education and the technical training of many who were formerly denied these privileges. The public libraries, which are dotting the country everywhere, have doors swinging easily at the touch of aspiration, admitting the mind of any toiler, who has the strength and time to make the effort, to companionship with the greatest minds of the ages. The moral obligation of taking thought for one's class, and for those interests which are vaster every way than the acquiring of an individual competence, is being increasingly recognized by the rank and file, and it is only a question of years until up out of the ranks there will come a much larger number of men of force and insight to furnish the necessary leadership so sorely demanded at this hour.

It is significant also that this ancient leader undertook his work, not in anger and hatred, but in the spirit of moral faith. Early in life the soul of Moses was stirred to its depths when he saw that Egyptian taskmaster beating the helpless slave. His blood was up in a moment, and in his fierce wrath he sprang upon the oppressor and killed him. But, although his cause was just, it is not in this mood that the real work of social deliverance can be wrought. God called him away at once into the wilderness, and there, through days and years of quiet meditation, of devotion and of useful labor, his nature ripened and matured until he had within him the true qualities of a deliverer. Now when he returned to Egypt, it was the coming of one who had put the shoes off his feet, because the place where he formed the high resolve to aid his people was holy ground. It was the coming of one who had seen the mysterious fire, which burns but does not consume, which removes the dross and leaves society fine and pure. It was the coming of one who had heard a voice from heaven saying, 'I am the God of Abraham, of Isaac, and of Jacob. I have seen the affliction of my people and have heard their cry by reason of their taskmasters, and I am come down to deliver them. Come, now, I will send thee, that thou mayest bring them out.' Moses came back, therefore, commissioned from on high, his face shining as the face of one who had seen God, for he had caught a vision of the divine sympathy for the struggling millions. He came back strong and serene in the consciousness of a high moral purpose, of a mission to aid in working out a divine ideal to which the power of heaven was openly pledged. " By faith he forsook Egypt, not fearing the wrath of the king, for he endured as seeing him who is invisible." It is in that nobler mood, and under the impulse of such moral faith, that the true work of social deliverance is to be undertaken.

The struggling people to-day will certainly be misled if they think that any permanent deliverance is to come through red-mouthed agitators who, casting aside the moral and spiritual, insist on making it merely a brute struggle for material advantage. They will be altogether misled if they think that breaking the wrists of men who refuse to belong to their industrial sect, or dynamiting the homes of men who insist upon the right to work, or destroying the property of those who will not be converted to their particular Gospel of Labor, will in any wise advance their interests. All this moral defiance and contempt for the spiritual, all this exaltation of anger and desperate reliance upon the fierce thrust of self-interest will surely fail, and it ought to fail. Before these blind impulses toward industrial relief can ever succeed, they, too, will have to go off into the wilderness of Midian, and keep sheep for forty years, until they learn the mood and temper in which social progress is made. They, too, must learn to put off their shoes as on holy ground, to face the bush that burns with fire in silent awe, and to hear the voice of Him who alone has the power and the wisdom to bring His twentieth-century people up out of the conditions where the lives of many are still made bitter and unfruitful by hard bondage.

Wide observation of the present industrial agitation and a careful perusal of a considerable amount of the literature of the labor movement have served to convince me that the tendency to-day is to expect altogether too much from the blind push of self-interest, and to lay altogether too little emphasis upon the results to be gained from the patient cultivation of that mutual regard which is deep-seated in all normally constituted men. It was the religious character of the Hebrew movement for industrial deliverance which uncovered deep wells of motive power for the furtherance of the work undertaken. The leaders of the enterprise were thus enabled, by the form which this ancient social effort took, to appeal successfully to those sentiments and aspirations which in all ages have shown themselves most effective in shaping history.

In the year 1855, six years before our Civil War, a hard-headed, practical man, whose name was David

Christy, wrote a book entitled " Cotton is King." He had no use for any foolish sentiment, he said. He took the hard facts of life as he found them, and he went on to show that the interests of the Southern cotton-growers demanded slavery if they were to prosper; and further, that the interests of the Northern manufacturers of cotton in the mills of Massachusetts and New York also demanded cheap cotton, which could best be produced by slave-labor in the South; and further, that the whole American people, wearing cotton clothing, most of them, every day in the year, demanded this same system of production; and that therefore the whole agitation about the abolition of slavery was but the troubled dream of a few silly enthusiasts. " Cotton is king," he said, " and it will finally determine the issue! "

But hard-headed, practical man though he was, he was utterly and eternally mistaken. Cotton was not king—love was king! Love of country and love of freedom, love of humanity and love of God—love was king even in that hour when David Christy was writing out his high claims about the kingship of cotton. And, indeed, before the ink was fairly dry upon the pages of his book, amid the rattle of mus-ketry and the roar of cannon, in the quiet tones of Lincoln's Inaugural Address and in the prayers of millions of people, the fundamental lordship of love was being effectively asserted. Men and women did great deeds in those days; they made great sacrifices; they carried through great enterprises, not because they were being paid for it in cotton—they were not paid for it at all. They did it because they loved —they loved their country, they loved liberty, they loved humanity, and they loved God more than any material advantage whatsoever. Love is king!

In our own day, we, also, have a saying on the street like unto that of David Christy's—it is to the effect that " Money talks." It means that money can say more, and can say it more effectively, in inspiring men to action, than any other voice. And this saying, likewise, sounds an utterly false note. Men will do and endure much for material gain, and they are doing it constantly. But when money comes out into the open and talks in the loudest tones it can command, its voice is altogether feeble as compared with the voice of love. The great deeds are still done, the great sacrifices are still made, the great burdens are still unflinchingly borne for love and not for gold.

All the year through, in peaceful walks of life no less than in war, the latent heroism in human nature is called out by love. Some months ago there was a wreck on the Baltimore and Ohio Railroad. Engineer Helgath was scalded to death, but in those last moments, while he was dying, he called to a passing brakeman, " Get a red lamp, somewhere, and go back and flag ' Forty-nine ' or she will be on top of us." He was not displaying this thoughtful heroism in the fearful agony of his dying condition for pay, but for love of his fellow-sufferers in the wreck. And in that same wreck, Nichols, the dining-car conductor, with both legs broken as well as several ribs, dragged himself along with his hands until, with a portion of his coat which he had torn off, he could plug the escape valve of the wrecked engine to prevent the escaping steam from scalding some imprisoned people. Love talks! Love says more, and says it more effectively, in all the great experiences of human life, than any other element we know. Love is king, and when we begin to show this supreme quality, we have openly allied ourselves with the strongest force on earth or in the sky for the winning of the victories that lie between us and our land of promise. It was love, in the highest manifestation of itself recorded anywhere in human history, which spoke out at the climax of its career and said in substance, " All power in heaven and on earth is, in the last anlysis, given unto me. Go ye therefore into all the world and conquer the nations by the power of this ultimate moral fact." Love is king, and those men are blind who would minimize its commanding influence.

There is to be a new crusade undertaken for the recovery of wide areas of Holy Land which Christ has made forever sacred by His loving interest. These holy fields are not away yonder where the Syrian stars look down—they are underneath our feet in those quarters where stand the mill, the factory, and the tenement-house. They are to be recovered from the hands of those Saracens who have seized them in selfishness, and who show more regard for brute force and for money power than for these moral principles and spiritual values. They are to be captured from those infidels who, by careless indifference to the well-being of others, as well as by the open rejection of Christ's commands, are trampling upon His cross. They are to be retaken from those who, by their defiance of Christian ideals, which are the traditional and legitimate ideals of American life, are become the enemies of our peace. Here in all our large cities and towns, some of these Saracens are encamped; it is imperative that a twentieth-century crusade should go boldly out against them, and it is for the Christian pulpit to furnish its full quota of competent leadership for this impending conflict.

The methods of Christian warfare, however, have radically changed since the twelfth century. The weapons of our warfare are not now carnal—they are intellectual and spiritual. These can be made mighty here in the land of the public school, the open ballot-box, and the free church, to the pulling down of strongholds. If these weapons, which are within the reach of all, can be wisely and justly used, they will prove sufficient for the recovery of our land to worthier occupancy. The land of Washington and of Lincoln, this " land of the pilgrims' pride, for which our fathers died," is altogether too holy to be permanently disgraced by organized and irresponsible selfishness. The forces which are to transform this narrow individualism, of which we have so much, into a habit of mind which looks sanely and sympathetically upon the things of others as well as upon its own, are not the bludgeon and the brickbat, not the pistol nor the bomb; they are the forces of instruction and persuasion—the forces which enlarge the mind, sanctify the heart and strengthen the will for the high and hard tasks imposed upon all men of intelligent good-will by present conditions.

I do not believe there is anything of overstatement in saying that the necessity now upon us as a people calls for just such a crusade in the interests of a higher righteousness. Are we not confronted by dangers which threaten the two most essential elements in the life of our Republic—equality before the law and freedom of opportunity for all men? Take the political party which is in power now, which has been in power for ten years, and which seems likely to remain in power for some years to come—is there not danger that it should be so controlled as to become the party of the strong and the privileged classes as against the helpless many? Splendid men there are in it—many of them —but these do not always find it easy to secure such action as will guard the interests of the common people against the injustice of the strong, the greedy, the irresponsible few.

There is also the willingness of people—north, south, east, and west—to allow what are supposed to be respectable corporations to corrupt city councils and legislatures and courts, for their own profit. Great public or semipublic utilities are administered for the gain of the few and to the sore loss of the many. Valuable franchises are secured for a song— if the song is only sung quietly, and to the muffled jingle of the guinea—and are then capitalized and utilized for unjust gain. The disposition on the part of many strong men to feel that they are above the law, and their readiness to employ certain skilful lawyers to see to it that those feelings are realized, is a solemn menace to the perpetuity of our free institutions. This whole tendency to allow the helpless to be trodden upon and the fortunate few to march over them into a showy success is perilous to the Republic.

Our most dangerous enemies to-day are not the low-browed criminals who occasionally rob the till of a store or break the head of some lonely passer-by in the street. These are only the mosquitoes of the jungle, annoying, destructive in some measure of our comfort, to be gotten rid of as fast as possible, but not deadly to the life of the nation. There are enemies of our peace who are as dangerous as the tigers in the jungle. They are the men who, by their wicked methods in commercial transactions, lower the tone of our national life, who puzzle and deaden the public conscience, who weaken the reverence for law by their higher lawlessness, who prostitute the sacred functions of government for their private ends—these are the tigers of the jungle, and they are dangerous. We have not yet learned how to deal with them as we have with the common ruffians who threaten the well-being of society with nothing more than occasional outbreaks of physical violence.

In grappling with these grievous problems, forced

upon us by the greed and the graft, by the fraud and the lust of modern times, there is a stern demand that our churches should be producing abundantly that same heroic stuff exhibited by our fathers at Valley Forge and Yorktown, at Shiloh and Gettysburg. Public spirit, uncalculating patriotism, readiness to sacrifice personal convenience to the demands of a higher service—all these are as requisite to-day as they have ever been in any great emergency of our national life:

> " Oh, beautiful my country, ours once more!
> What were our lives without thee?
> What all our lives to save thee?
> We reck not what we give thee;
> We will not dare to doubt thee;
> But ask whatever else, and we will dare."

The religious motive for this new crusade against irresponsible self-interest will be found, in my judgment, in the more thorough application of the principles involved in the truth of the Incarnation. The transfer of the centre of theological thought from the Atonement to the Incarnation has been frequently remarked upon in the more thoughtful reviews. The reconciliation of the individual sinner to his Maker and the salutary provisions for his well-being in a future world, considered quite apart from his obligations to those industrial and political relations in which he stands, does not now hold the centre of the stage as it once did. The sacredness of human life here and now, as viewed in the light of the Incarnation, makes imperative an unceasing effort to provide for all the children of men an environment that shall facilitate and not hinder their approach toward that high norm of spiritual excellence revealed and made possible for humanity through Jesus of Nazareth. His splendid statement, " I am the vine, ye are the branches," opens up a noble vista of unparalleled opportunity to the aspiring soul, and it also imposes the weightiest obligation the conscience can feel touching those lives which are, by their unhappy surroundings, almost inevitably thrust away from any real fellowship with the spiritual energy there named for the redemption of humanity. The sense of duty which springs from our recognition of the fact that social conditions to a great degree make or mar men, thus showing themselves potent in saving or in destroying spiritual life, is wonderfully strengthened when it is viewed in the light which streams from this great truth of the Incarnation.

Resuming the narrative again, you will notice the form of sanction to be placed upon this second saner and truer effort of Moses for the deliverance of the oppressed Israelites. " This shall be a sign that I have sent thee; when thou hast brought my people out, they shall *serve me* upon this mountain." The result of industrial betterment was to be found not so much in the increase of material advantage as in their service of God through a higher, holier life. It was more, much more, than a mere question of bread and butter—the sign of victory was to be seen in the changed characters of those who profited by this deliverance undertaken in the spirit of moral faith. They would come up out of the struggle to " serve God " as they had never served Him before.

This is the Gospel of Labor as recorded in the Old Testament, and that which stands recorded in the New Testament is like unto it. " Come unto me all ye that labor and are heavy laden," said the Carpenter Prophet who came out of Nazareth, " and I will give you rest." He nowhere promised the rest of fat and sleek material prosperity, nor the rest of well-fed indifference to the spiritual values of life. He offered them the rest of a higher allegiance and of a holier form of service. This genuine rest was to be found by " taking His yoke " upon the weary shoulders and by " learning from Him " that way of life which would bring peace to the soul. It was with the same high purpose that this ancient labor leader came from the spot that was holy ground, from the bush that burned with a mysterious fire, and from his conference with a divine presence, to bring the people out—it was all done that they might the more worthily serve God. " This shall be the sign that I have sent thee, when thou hast brought my people out, they shall ' serve me ' upon this mountain."

The gigantic difficulties in his way when he undertook the deliverance can readily be pictured. Here was a mass of uninstructed, unorganized slaves, superstitious and timid regarding any effort to disturb the existing order. The feeling that it was better to let well enough alone was strong upon them, as we shall see later, even when the " well enough " was an oriental slavery. The venture of any attempt at change frightened them, for the reason that their unaspiring minds were sadly deficient in that spiritual imagination which can picture to itself better conditions to be secured by obeying the upthrust of wholesome discontent, which is commonly the push of a divine purpose resident within. The strength of Pharaoh and the power of resistance apparent in the system of oppression then in vogue were enough to dishearten this industrial leader, but added to all that was the apathy and irresponsiveness of the people he would serve.

We had a fairly correct reproduction of it several years ago in the situation among the anthracite miners in Pennsylvania, when their leaders began to grapple with that problem. The coal operators in that field had been insistent upon a high tariff, to "protect American industry" they said, and were meanwhile assisting in the immigration of Poles and Hungarians, Austrians and Italians of the lower type to beat down the rate of wages in Pennsylvania by an oversupply of labor near the industries they conducted. There were at that time about one hundred and forty-seven thousand coal miners at work there, on such hard terms that great numbers of English and Scotch, German and Welsh miners had been driven out because of their inability to compete with that lower standard of living. For a term of years these unorganized men had been suffering injustice in long hours and low wages; in unjust "docking" and exorbitant charges for the powder used, which was furnished from the company stores; from an average yearly employment of only one hundred and eleven days, as the commission appointed by President Roosevelt discovered; and from a scale of living too low to be called human. The haughty attitude of the operators, who refused to meet the representatives of the men when they were finally gotten together in an organization,

saying, " We have nothing to arbitrate," was dis-
heartening, but even more trying was the despondent, distracted feeling among the miners themselves. The dull, sodden material with which the
prophet or reformer must oftentimes deal in working
out his aspiration into genuine accomplishment becomes one of the most serious impediments to the
progress of any worthy movement.

But the very gravity of the situation and the huge
obstacles standing in the way of advance make the
call for inspired and unselfish leadership all the
more imperative. They act as a challenge to the
heroic stuff which must enter into the composition
of any man worthy to hold the prophetic office.
They are like the Master's words to those two aspiring young men who were eager to sit, one upon
His right hand and the other upon His left. " Can
ye drink the cup that I drink, and be baptized with
the baptism I am baptized with? " He asked them.
The very challenge embodied in His words summoned
into action their moral reserves—in words of ringing confidence they replied, " We can! " It was,
indeed, " the venture of faith," the sense of joyous
reliance upon those unseen aids which would sustain them as supporting allies, which thus led them
to accept the call to hard service. And in terms
no less searching, you, too, as young men who are

candidates for the Christian ministry, will be called upon to drink the cup of willing sacrifice and to be baptized with power from on high, in order that you may furnish your full share of moral leadership in this work of social advance.

CHAPTER V

THE whole industrial framework in which those ancient Israelites found themselves in the days of Moses was so filled with injustice and oppression that their divinely appointed leader regarded it as useless to hope for spiritual progress on their part until that environment was changed. But the prevailing system was greatly to the advantage of Pharaoh and his nobles, and they would naturally rally to its defence. The whole superstructure of society in that part of Egypt, resting as it did economically upon the unrequited labor of those slaves, was in great measure dependent for its ease upon the continuance of the existing *régime*. The social order thus intrenched and fortified seemed altogether too strong to be radically altered by any effort of the oppressed people themselves. Moses therefore decided that the only way of advance lay in the transfer of the Israelites to some new field.

The same stern necessity for radical modification of the existing order obtains now in many situations

145

where spiritual progress is still effectively hindered by the evils inherent in that order. The people who suffer from these wrong conditions cannot gain relief by emigrating to some other country, for all modern countries are under the same stress. Relief can only come as all hands take hold together to accomplish what those Egyptians should have accomplished on behalf of the oppressed Israelites who were suffering because of wrong industrial methods, viz., eliminate the evils of an iniquitous system. If a captive sailor on a pirate ship, who had been given the enforced option of walking the plank or joining the thieving crew, would undertake to become a Christian and live a right life, he must either leave that ship or else address himself to the hard task of changing its whole method and purpose. He could not remain a consenting member of such a crew, participating in the rewards of such a system, and keep his conscience clear or make any sort of spiritual headway. It matters not to what extent he might strive to cultivate an individual and private piety— he might sing hymns, read his Bible, and pray with all the earnestness and regularity imaginable—he would not in this way obtain spiritual peace, while he allowed the piratical order which brought him his daily bread to remain unattacked.

I purposely choose a glaring illustration—it is not

put forward as an accurate picture of existing conditions—but the essential principle indicated in my use of it is altogether sound and may be extensively applied. If some of the prevalent industrial methods actually prevent men from rendering obedience to the teachings of Christ, must not these men also either get out or strive to change the evil features of the system? Conscientious business men to-day in declining the minister's invitation to join the church frequently assign as their reason that under present conditions they cannot undertake to obey Christ. The man who is conducting a large department-store, which makes gain by selling certain articles below cost for a definite period until smaller concerns in that line have been crushed out of existence, and who feels compelled to that course by the current competitive methods, finds it difficult to render any proper obedience to the Golden Rule. The manufacturer, who follows the way of the world in fixing the rate of wages for his factory hands, and who, because of the stern pressure of a system, does not quite see how he could do otherwise, is somewhat confused at being told that a fundamental demand of Christ is that we love our neighbors as ourselves. These examples might be multiplied indefinitely, and they make plain this truth, that the essential spirit of the organized life itself must be changed if the individuals concerned in it are to live a properly regenerate life. It was not the purpose of Jesus that live men should be taken out of the world, but that they should be delivered from the evil of it; and there is consequently an insistent demand for better methods which will make it possible for good men in their every-day work to live out the love they feel for their fellows.

Employers and employés alike are under the stress of an unnatural pressure. The actual yearly wage of many working-men compels them to adopt a style of living not adapted to mental or moral growth. And even with this low standard it is a constant struggle to secure enough to satisfy their actual needs. Life becomes an unceasing effort to avoid open, painful, degrading poverty. And on the other hand, many of the employers of these same men are themselves in a life-and-death struggle to avoid bankruptcy. The mercantile agencies tell us that something like ninety per cent of all the men who go into business fail at some time during their commercial history. The man who enters business with a true Christian purpose is compelled to compete with men who are not embarrassed by any such scruples. He is sometimes driven to make his choice between adopting the current methods, or going out of business, or making financial failure. The more generous conduct of his own business may mean that he will be undersold by some sharp competitor; and because many people will always buy where they can buy cheapest, regardless of other considerations, he may find himself thrust to the wall for his pains. All this shows that there is something wrong with the spirit of the system.

Furthermore, is it possible to-day, under present conditions, to stand up and tell an audience of working-people what Jesus told His hearers? "Be not anxious for the morrow as to what ye shall eat or what ye shall drink or wherewithal ye shall be clothed: seek ye first the kingdom of God, and all these things shall be added unto you." Be not anxious? Thousands of them under present conditions must be anxious! They can see for themselves that many sober, frugal, industrious wage-earners work all their lives, barely meeting the inevitable expenses, haunted all the while with the fear of accident, illness, or death in their families, which would bring obligations they would not know how to meet. And during those active years there is stealing on the inevitable old age, with the clear possibility of loss of work because of inability to longer keep the pace. Seeking the kingdom of God as an experience of personal piety will not surely bring them a competence. The kingdom of God, which is to be sought by them and by us and by all hands taking hold together, is a much larger affair than individual and private piety. It includes such a reorganization of the industrial forces and such an equitable use of the resources placed at our command, as shall make it possible for all right-minded and industrious people to gain those necessary supplies without constant and distressing anxiety.

There has been a feeling prevalent in the minds of many religious people that these efforts to modify the existing environment have in them a certain worldly and secular element; and that they therefore lie somewhat outside the field of true religious effort. The church has, in long periods of its history, been deficient in its attention to the influence of environment upon character, and its reluctance, when urged to coöperate with other agencies for the improvement of physical surroundings, has been to its discredit. Scientific research has demonstrated that, given time enough and a slowly changing environment, water-breathing, marine forms of life can be actually changed into air-breathing land forms— and this without the introduction of any modifying influences other than those resident in the environment. It will be made clear in due time, by a more thorough study of the influence registered by surrounding conditions upon spiritual unfolding, that this radical physical transformation has its counterpart in the world of moral values.

The Master clearly recognized the power of environment. Right in the forefront of that series of parables touching the coming kingdom He set " the Parable of the Soil," as it is correctly styled.   In the varying fortunes of the seed, cast as it was into varying soils, He portrayed the conditioning power of physical surroundings upon spiritual progress. The one who sowed the good seed, He said, was " the Son of man," yet even where the germs of new life fell from the perfect hand of the Incarnate One Himself, the hope of a harvest was either destroyed or sadly blighted where the seed fell into weedy or into stony or into shallow soil.   And even where the seed fell into good soil, fit and prepared for the purpose, the varying fertility of that good soil made inevitable a varying harvest, here thirty-fold, there sixty, and only in exceptional spots as much as a hundred-fold.   This parable of the soil, set out in the very foreground of those parables which portray the methods of the unfolding spiritual kingdom which Jesus came to establish, makes plain the duty of His church to give more serious and radical attention than has been its custom during long stretches of its history, to the direct bearing of social environment upon moral character.

The effort of the church has too often been directed exclusively to the regeneration of the individual considered quite apart from that system of things in which he was a consenting or maybe a controlling item. Some evangelists have steadily preached as if the two texts in the Bible to be taken literally, and to be urged with all possible vigor, were these: " Except a man be born again he cannot see the kingdom of God," and " Believe on the Lord Jesus Christ and thou shalt be saved "; those extensive portions of Scripture which deal with social interests being treated apparently as if they were all more or less figurative, or else simply explanatory of the one idea of individual piety. But Jesus preached constantly " the kingdom of God," not merely as a mode of personal experience, but still more as a new social order to be attained by men acting together in His spirit. It has been justly said that many people have been more ready to trust Jesus to deliver them from the hell of which He spoke but rarely, than to believe Him competent to establish that finer social order on which He dwelt habitually in His utterances regarding the kingdom. The need for His larger message is apparent in the fact that there are to-day vast numbers of regenerate people, devoted and sincere as to those duties which belong to personal piety, who are nevertheless steadily causing trouble by social wrong-doing and who are uninterested in the more radical efforts to cure it because of their defective sense of social responsibility.

This " kingdom," of which Jesus said so much, was not a mere subjective experience of the soul, nor was it simply a perfect rule of life for the individual. In fact, about the only expression which gives any countenance to such a view is the statement, " The kingdom of heaven is within you," or, more properly, as in the Revised Version, " among you "—indicating that the beginnings of the new social order were already present. The kingdom is represented as something objective—a mustard-seed growing gradually into a mighty tree, a mass of meal permeated by a new principle, a wedding feast entered upon in the right spirit, a company of laborers in a vineyard dominated by loyalty to an unseen Master and by fraternal feeling for one another. The kingdom of heaven is an objective fact and not a mere inner experience.

This kingdom was not a distant state to which men were to go at death—the kingdom was to come; it was to come down, like a holy city out of heaven, finding its secure foundations in nobler conditions of earthly life as these came to be dominated by the spirit of the Master. " By the kingdom of God

Jesus meant," according to Shailer Mathews, " an ideal social order in which the relations of men to God should be that of sons, and to each other that of brothers." In such an order the cruel inequalities, the hopeless struggles of the weak, the savage selfishness sometimes manifested in industrial life, would inevitably vanish. This new social environment, then, made up of renewed men and of institutions which should embody the spirit and method of the Master, into which every child should be born as into his native element for the realization of his true life, men were to seek first; and in the gaining of it, all these things, food, drink, raiment, and the rest, would indeed be added to every industrious soul without the fret and care of a consuming anxiety.

The entire impression which any fair-minded man without previous theological bias would get in reading the four gospels would be that Jesus never regarded the world as in any sense a wreck. He was not seeking to get a few men off of it, and out of it, and, by their individual piety, safely up into heaven. He regarded this present world as a ship which the human race could learn to sail and on which they could maintain an existence worthy to be esteemed a high privilege to every soul aboard. He saw that many were still sea-sick and uncomfortable; many were being bruised and broken by movements to which they had not adjusted themselves; many were frightened and anxious, the greater part of the time, as to their personal safety. But all this was to be temporary—they were to learn how to make such assignments of duty, how to organize such a ship's crew, and how to adjust matters for everybody aboard as to make the voyage of life safe, inspiring, and joyous. This I believe to be the main trend of the teaching of Jesus in His utterances regarding the kingdom; and it surely furnishes us with high scriptural warrant for our attempt to correct the evils of environment and for expecting the actual regeneration of society itself.

But for those oppressed Israelites, to whom I must return, without possessions or recognized rights, without experience or any considerable insight, opposed as they were by an old, rich, and powerful *régime* there in the valley of the Nile, the only hope of any radical improvement in outward condition lay in flight. There was a providential preparation for such a movement in a series of public calamities which at that time befell the land of Egypt. The form these calamities took was such as to humble and dishearten the oppressors, until in their desperation they were actually ready to allow the slaves to go free. The calamities were also of such a character as to produce a conviction in the minds of the

Israelites that the Supreme Power behind all phenomena was strongly enlisted on their side; and this
assurance begat in them, for brief periods at least,
a real confidence that a freer and nobler life was
indeed within their reach.

The water of the Nile ran red as blood, as if
stained with guilt by the oppression along its shores.
The annual overflow of the river was followed by
the spawning of frogs upon the wet fields in such
unprecedented numbers that they became an offence.
As the season wore on, myriads of lice, and then of
flies, and then of locusts, came upon all the face of
Egypt, destroying alike the comfort of men and the
harvests of the field. A grievous disease or murrain
broke out among the cattle; an epidemic of boils,
or, as it would probably be termed to-day, bubonic
plague, ran its fearful course among men. Still later
one of those sand-storms, which sometimes darken
the sky until one can scarcely see his hand before
him, swept in from the desert, and the city on the
Nile groped in a darkness that could be felt. And
then a hail-storm of extraordinary severity stripped
the trees of their foliage, the fields of their crops,
and even destroyed the lives of men and of beasts.
All these visitations came with a certain cumulative
effect in a progressive intensity. The narrative as
it stands seems to be the work of an author who, as a

genuine artist, gathered up, summarized, and put in striking literary form the accounts of a long series of calamities, which stretched out, it maybe, over many years. He did it that he might give dramatic statement to this truth, that God's judgments fall heavily and steadily upon social injustice and selfish inhumanity.

The calamities themselves, when we study them carefully, are seen to bear a close relationship to the environment, for it is the divine habit to use materials already at hand in the accomplishment of its purposes. The water of the Nile, in modern times, has occasionally, by the unusual deposit of sediment and red clay, been rendered unfit for use. In the wet season frogs, and in the dry season flies and lice and locusts have come occasionally in unprecedented numbers, even as the grasshoppers became a perfect scourge in our own Kansas for two successive years, and then came again no more. So the sand-storm and the hail, the murrain and the bubonic plague, are not unknown in the life of that land. Providence uses means already at hand, as Jesus indicated, when, in His classic illustration of God's kindly care, He pointed to the clothing of the lilies and the feeding of the birds, not by a succession of miracles, or by any miracle at all, but through the constant operation of those great natural agencies which stand as an abiding expression of God's interest in all that He has made.

It is one of the limitations of some of the Old Testament writers that they were inclined to make the connection between wrong-doing and all manner of misfortune so clear and so close as sometimes to overreach themselves. We find this weak spot in their theological system pointed out and discussed at length in the Book of Job, as well as in other parts of the Scriptures. But the man who suffered such dire misfortune in the land of Uz was not an evil-doer—he was a sound, straight, God-fearing, evil-hating man—and some truer explanation of the calamities which befell him had to be found. The men on whom the tower of Siloam fell were not sinners above all the men in Jerusalem; nor was a certain man born blind because of exceptional wickedness on the part of his parents. There are unsolved questions and puzzling remainders in the ordering of the physical world which present insight cannot fully explain. We shall fall into many an error if we insist upon connecting every great disaster, like that of the destruction of San Francisco by earthquake and fire, with some wrong-doing on the part of those who directly suffer from it.

Yet the true moral content of this narrative of the ten plagues is absolutely sound. It will not always be found true that a ruler or a slave-owner or an employer guilty of injustice and cruelty will be overtaken by precisely such calamities as are here described—by hail-stones and darkness, by flies and frogs, by lice and locusts, by grievous boils and deadly murrain—this may or may not be so. But it is forever true that selfish inhumanity in organized life will be overtaken by industrial darkness and storm; it will be stung and bitten by myriads of petty annoyances; it will be made sick and sore by the outbreak of social disease. And what is more serious than all this, the effect of inhuman and oppressive methods upon the man himself who is guilty of them, and upon his children, is disastrous beyond anything here suggested in this narrative of physical calamities. The sore plagues of the divine disapproval fasten themselves in moral blight upon such a man's household. In that utter defeat of the dearest hopes of some family which has grown rich by taking unfair advantage of the helpless—a defeat frequently witnessed in modern society—we see written in a plain hand the stern rebuke of the Almighty Himself. God's judgments upon the contempt men show for the high ideals He holds before them come now in one form and now in another—the chariots which bear the divine penalties are twenty thousand —but they surely come, and the stately procession of His great rebukes is never long delayed. Down through the ages He has been steadily calling to those men who were dealing harshly with their helpless fellows, " Let my people go, that they may serve me; if thou refuse, I will smite all thy borders."

We have here in our own country at this time what is often called " the white plague," the disease known as tuberculosis of the lungs. All the deaths from cholera and small-pox, from diphtheria and scarlet-fever, sink into insignificance when compared with the steady ravages of tuberculosis. In the United States alone there were one hundred and fifty thousand deaths last year from this dread disease, and at the present time there are, according to the tabulated reports of the State boards of health, one million two hundred and fifty thousand cases of tuberculosis in this country of ours. If the present ratio is kept up, ten millions out of the eighty millions composing the population of our country will die from this one disease—that is, one in every eight of all our people will fall a victim to tuberculosis. The peril which confronts society in the presence of these myriads of death-dealing germs is one of the gravest problems in modern medical science.

And when the Tenement-House Commission in the City of New York made its report some time ago, among the many items of vital importance they noted the fact that there were twenty thousand consumptives in the tenement-houses of New York alone. Each consumptive can, we are told, expectorate in a day seven millions of germs or bacilli. These sputa from the diseased lungs dry and are afterward blown about in the dust through the tenement-houses, and in the streets, in the theatres, street-cars and railway trains, as well as into offices, factories, and the open windows of the well-to-do. These germs are soon killed by sunshine, but they live, as a frightful menace to health, for months together, in damp or in dark places. These poor consumptives in the tenement district have not been carefully instructed regarding their social responsibility as possessors of such a disease; and even had they been, they might not unnaturally feel that, inasmuch as society has shown so little care for their interests, it is not imperative that they should exercise the utmost caution touching the public health. There they work on from sheer necessity in the sweat shops of the great city, making neckties, cheap boys' clothing, and underwear for the trade. There they sit breathing out disease and stitching it into the garments they make, sending out the germs of death broadcast over the land! The cast-off skin of some rattlesnake would be a clean and wholesome garment as compared with this sweat-shop clothing, which pious merchants, for a sufficient consideration, sometimes buy and sell, with the sentence of death woven into its very fibre. The close quarters and the foul air, the insufficient food and the cold, damp rooms, because fuel is high and wages are small, all serve to make these workrooms admirable culture grounds for these germs of disease, which are to be speedily sent out into half the States of the Union.

And what does all this frightful menace to the national health mean but a modern embodiment of the truth contained in that old Exodus narrative. God be praised for microbes and bacilli! They are great promoters of human sympathy and of the sense of social responsibility. They preach the gospel of brotherhood far and wide, saying, in such tones that people are bound to sit up and listen, "We are all members one of another; if one neglected member suffer, all the other members may, by reason of these very germs, be called upon to suffer with it." Out of those wretched tenements, with their pinched faces, narrow chests, and hollow coughs, the voice of God comes, and it says again as it said of old, "Deliver my people from these inhuman conditions; if thou shalt refuse, I will smite all thy borders with the white plague."

And it is to be remembered, also, that this menace to physical well-being is but an outward and visible symbol of an inward and spiritual peril which threatens the souls of those who are content to live on indifferent to the needs and claims of their less fortunate fellows. Upon them and upon their children, wherever they can justly be held responsible for conditions which work injury to the helpless, there comes the blight of a moral tuberculosis which works frightful and lasting havoc upon the more precious interests of the inner life!

In the long run it is a very just old world we live in. Pay-day does not come every Saturday night, nor do the Lord's harvests recur each year, but they all come! Just as sure as sunrise and sunset, whatsoever men and nations and systems sow, that—not some fancy substitute for it, but that—shall they also reap! The house or the industry or the national life built upon the practice of hearing these sayings of Christ and doing them, stands. And the house or the industry or the national life built upon the practice of hearing these sayings of His and doing them not, falls under the combined attack of the winds and the waves which are sure to come and beat upon it.

Up out of the Nile, flowing red, as if guilty of the blood of the helpless slaves along its banks; back from the wet swamps where crawled the myriads of frogs; down from the upper air where fluttered the locusts of destruction; straight out of the desert, with its sand-storm and darkness, came these symbols of powerful and unending opposition to selfish inhumanity! The real content of this narrative is altogether applicable to the conditions of life in any period of the world's history, for God is perpetually and relentlessly at war with all injustice and oppression. Still the divine voice cries out, "Deliver my helpless people that they may glorify me; if thou refuse, I will smite all thy borders."

These particular calamities which fell upon Egypt were of such a nature that they struck directly at the heart of Pharaoh and of his whole system of faith and practice as well. It was no ordinary river which became vile and unfit to drink; it was, as Stanley says, "the sacred, solitary, beneficent Nile, the life of the state and the source of all fertility," the object of a reverence almost worshipful. It was upon no common race of men but upon "the cleanliest of all ancient people" that there came the flies and the lice, the stench of the frogs and the plague of boils. It was no ordinary region which failed in its harvest, but the rich and sure Nile delta, which was riddled by the hail-storms and swept clean by the locusts. It was not merely the common beasts of the field but the sacred bull Apis that groaned under the grievous murrain. When these calamities fell upon the land Pharaoh no longer seemed to himself or to his subjects to be the favored of heaven and the darling of the gods—he seemed to be mocked and beaten by some mysterious foe. There are, indeed, penalties for wrong-doing which neither wealth nor royal influence is able to ward off. There are enemies of our peace which enter the home and the heart without ever asking leave, and they cannot be expelled by anything less than penitence, new purpose, and the divine forgiveness.

Pharaoh was at first inclined to humble himself in penitence and to undertake a new life. He sent for Moses and said: "I have sinned; the Lord is righteous and I and my people are wicked. Entreat the Lord that there be no more plagues and I will let Israel go." But, "when Pharaoh saw that the hail and thundering were ceased, he sinned yet more and hardened his heart." When the pain stopped, like many a modern sufferer, he turned again to the old life of luxury and oppression. "The devil is sick, the devil a monk would be! The devil is well "—you will recall the rest of it. Pharaoh hardened his heart; there came a stiffening of the will, a fresh opposition to the divine appeal. And this operation was repeated until moral opposition to the will of God and an inhuman indifference to the needs of his fellows became his settled character. When God's rebukes and entreaties are persistently scorned the inevitable result is to fix the character in opposition to His holy will; and, finally, between that soul and the holier life once possible "there is a great gulf fixed" which cannot in any wise be crossed. Pharaoh became stubborn in disobedience, yet he was haunted perpetually by an awful fear that he was under the displeasure of some mysterious and supernatural foe.

The courage of the oppressed Israelites, on the other hand, grew mightily during these painful calamities. A power not of man seemed to be hurling its effective rebukes against their oppressors. The huge system which held them in its grasp had seemed too powerful to be overthrown, but now it was shaken like a reed in the wind, by this forerunner of a brighter day. The various events as they occurred were interpreted to them by their leader Moses—and they felt the full force of it when he said, "The Lord shall fight for you and ye shall hold your peace." The great Ally did indeed seem to be drawing up His forces, tempest and darkness, plague and pestilence, disease and death. He was setting them all in battle-array against Pharaoh and his host. The hour of deliverance seemed to be drawing nigh. The Israelites began to actually believe in that unseen Friend who, years before, out of the midst of a bush which burned with a strange fire, had declared His far-reaching purpose. " I am the God of Abraham, of Isaac, and of Jacob. I have seen the affliction of my people; I have heard their cry by reason of their taskmasters and I am come down to deliver them." Surely that great fulfilment was at hand; and, finally, when Pharaoh's first-born son, the heir to the throne of Egypt, died, and when other deaths throughout the land had filled the masters of those slaves with a mighty dread, Moses called upon the people to rise and follow him in a splendid effort for their freedom. They responded to his call, and in an hour of high resolve and splendid faith they actually threw off their bondage and set out for the land of promise.

How far away it might be none of those ignorant toilers knew. How all the intervening country was to be traversed they could not say. How the many problems involved in the occupation of new territory, and in the establishment of a new social order were to be solved, not even Moses could have told. They only knew that they were oppressed and were not living human lives. They believed that the Great Ally had something better in store for them, and was pledged to its realization. And with that feeling of sore need, and in that hope of divine help, they started.

Those sagacious people who tell us that no minister of the gospel, no reformer, no student of social conditions ought to speak in public about these serious and difficult problems which confront us in our modern industrial system until he knows just what ought to be done and just how it can be done, have certainly failed to read their Bibles. No man knows all this! But shall we go on maintaining an inactive silence until we know all the windings of the pathway to better conditions? The oppression of the helpless is a fact. The call for deliverers sounds from bushes which burn with the fire of social sympathy on all the hillsides of modern life. The careless indifference of many, whose fortunate lives make them unmindful of the toiling multitude on whose bare shoulders rests the burden of their own showy, useless luxury, is one of the moral reproaches of modern civilization. The fact that social disaster and wide-spread calamity follow upon selfish inhumanity is plain to all who have eyes to see! Can men of insight and conscience, then, possibly hold their peace until, forsooth, they know the final solution? They cannot know as yet what that better substitute for the present system shall be—they must go forward feeling their way as did these Is-

raelites of old. Uncertain as they are on many
points, unable as they are to outline a complete programme for the social advance, they still take up
and echo the same cry, " Speak unto the children of
Israel that they go forward," in the quest of a freer
and a fuller life.

It was imperative that there should be some radical change in the environment of those oppressed
people before the purpose of God could be fulfilled
for them, and the same moral necessity for an improved social environment rests upon society to-day.
It matters not how highly we may exalt the commanding influence of a regenerate life upon the prevailing conditions in the social order where that
individual life is set down, we cannot avoid the truth
that the world without perpetually lays a strong
hand of influence upon the life within. We find the
recognition of this truth in the method of that Eternal Purpose which stretched across the ages, in the
selection of a time and place for that supreme manifestation which God has made of Himself in the
person of His Son. When the Son of God was born
into the world He was " born in Bethlehem of Judea,
for thus it was written by the prophets." He was
born into an environment which a providential purpose had been patiently preparing during all those
preceding centuries of unique spiritual experiences

wrought out in the life of a chosen people. He was born, too, when conditions were favorable for the establishment of His kingdom. "In the fulness of time, God sent His Son," for the prevalence of peace at that time, the unifying of the world around the Mediterranean under the rule of the Roman Empire, the wide diffusion of the Greek language as a fitting instrument for the conveyance of spiritual truth, and other circumstances in the environment, all combined to make the Advent timely and promising. We have in the very time and place and manner of Christ's entrance into this world, testimony borne from on high as to the abiding spiritual significance of environment.

Those who lay the entire burden of the world's advance upon individual regeneration are endeavoring to row their boat with but one oar, and the inevitable circling about on their track ensues. It has become the settled conviction of many minds that slavish deference to the law of supply and demand, and the habit of ignoring the human values, which so largely prevails in many modern industries, effectually block the way of spiritual advance for the men involved. Employers cannot go on hiring men for the lowest wages they will consent to take without asking as to the effect of such a wage on the standard of living; they cannot go on encouraging the immigration of large numbers of cheap laborers to the vicinity of a certain industry, that wages may be forced down and kept down by cruel competition among the men; they cannot continue to discharge men with families to support, when boys and girls can be hired to do the work at a lower wage, never inquiring as to the effect of such action upon those families. This whole habit of ignoring the law of Christ and the consideration that men owe to one another renders such a social group not much better indeed than a ship's company of far-seeing, hard-hearted pirates. No amount of money given, out of the rewards of an industry so conducted, to charity to care for the unfortunate lives rendered helpless largely by the industry itself, can ever atone for a lack of resolute effort by the responsible parties to make the work of the world, no less than its worship and its charity, an expression of the spirit of Jesus Christ.

When these Israelites undertook to secure for themselves a more wholesome environment, they made their start, as was natural, in the darkness and cool of the night. Out from the scenes where they had suffered in mind and body, out of those conditions which had meant the enfeeblement of the higher purpose and the dwarfing of their spiritual natures, they marched away toward the place of freedom. Uncertain as to almost all of the steps to be taken ultimately, they still went forward, feeling within their hearts a divine impulse which became to them at last as a pillar of cloud by day and of fire by night.

The next evening they were one day's march upon the road, and when night fell they were encamped by a narrow arm of the Red Sea. "The Lord led them not by the way of the land of the Philistines," the narrator tells us, "although that was near." The short cut would have brought them to their new responsibilities without the requisite preparatory training; and this might have brought defeat to the entire undertaking. Such a course would have been as ill-advised as are the ready-made programmes and panaceas for social ills sometimes offered to-day, which similarly leave out of account the necessity for the gradual development of the higher type of man needed for the working of the new *régime* proposed. The Israelites therefore were divinely commanded to take the long road, which meant years of patient effort in the wild life of the rugged steppes, which included also a long and educative encampment at the foot of Mount Sinai, to the end that they might be trained and fitted for the obligations which would face them when they actually reached the land of promise.

Here before them, then, at the close of the first day's march, lay the arm of the sea, the dividing line between the old life and the new. To cross this boundary was to pass from Africa into Asia; to pass from Egypt, with its mighty river and huge structures, its significant bull-worship and grinding oppression, its elaborate, burdensome, unprogressive civilization, over into Asia, the home of spiritual ideals, the cradle of all the great religions of the world. Abraham, the father of Judaism, had come up out of the valley of the Euphrates, in Asia, to establish the faith of their fathers! Gautama, the rich young nobleman, sat for six long years, silent and thoughtful, under the bo-tree, and then, by his great renunciation, founded Buddhism in Asia! Confucius, whose teaching still moulds the lives of millions in populous China, was a man of Asia! Mohammed came up from Arabia, in Asia, to preach the religion of the Koran, next to our own the most powerful and aggressive religion the world has ever known! And Jesus of Nazareth, who has taken the moral government of the world upon His shoulder as none other has in all the ages, was born in Bethlehem of Judea, there on the western coast of Asia!

Asiatics they were, one and all, these leaders and founders of the world's historic faiths! Israel in crossing the arm of the Red Sea was moving over into the seat and home of the great religions. Much of this splendid history which I have indicated was yet to be enacted, but the spirit of Him who is from everlasting to everlasting looked out of the cloud that day upon the scattered hosts, and He saw the mighty significance of the event, when the Hebrews made ready to cross the Red Sea from Africa into Asia.

How much it meant for them to emerge, crude and untaught though they were, into a realm of spiritual ideals! In the slavery of Egypt there was no vision and the higher life of the people perished. But in the land of promise, while it was a long, slow process—first the blade, then the ear, then, at a long remove, the full corn in the ear—they were brought under the appeal of the priest and the lawgiver, of the poet and the prophet! They were brought under the influence of men of spiritual insight, who led their minds on and up to the point where they established relationships with the Unseen. Commonplace though their lives were, as they wandered in the desert, as they fought for a footing in Canaan, and as they developed their institutions in the peaceful occupation of the land the Lord their God had given them, there was steady growth as they discovered the deeper significance of those common interests, as they related them to a far-reaching divine purpose, as they saw the transcendent possibilities of the lives they were living through the mighty leadership to which they had become attached.

They were also passing from a condition of slavery, where the responsibility for their support rested with others, to a state of freedom, where the responsibility would become their own. They were crossing from the complexity of a civilization which puzzled and burdened them to the simplicity of a life with which they were more competent to deal. They were forsaking the fat delta of the Nile, with its leeks and onions, its melons and its cucumbers, for the rugged life and scantier fare of the steppes. It was indeed a night much to be observed and long to be remembered, because of its vital bearing upon the destiny of this people, who were then striking their initial blow for industrial deliverance. It is only natural that some of the prominent features in this notable experience should have been enshrined and commemorated in the Jewish Feast of Passover, which has endured through all the ages to this very hour.

There on the shore of the Red Sea, then, they paused in their flight and pitched their camp. But as the sun went down behind the western sand-hills, a cloud of dust rose upon the horizon, and presently they saw in the distance the horses and chariots of Pharaoh's army in hot pursuit. The loss of an abundant supply of cheap labor had been instantly felt by the ruling class; the calamities had all passed and the sky had cleared; and now the army was ordered out to bring those Israelites back and fix them again in hard bondage. The dust of the pursuers in their forced march rose upon the horizon as the sun went down, and the Israelites were sore afraid.

Instantly there went up a great cry against Moses, and against the whole undertaking for industrial betterment. Let danger or difficulty arise and the fickle, faint-hearted people will commonly cry out against the folly of all such attempts. " Were there not graves enough in Egypt," they shouted to their leader, " that thou hast brought us to die by the sword in the wilderness? " It was a bitter taunt— " not graves enough in Egypt," that land of tombs, where interest in the dead all but overshadowed interest in the living, even as the Pyramids of the dead towered above the homes of the living! Horrible slaughter for all who did not instantly submit seemed inevitable as the chariots of Pharaoh's army swept toward them across the sands. And for those who might survive there seemed no better fate than hard bondage again, with the tale of bricks once more doubled as a penalty for attempted revolt.

But Moses sought to reassure them by his confident promise of divine aid. They were surely obeying an impulse from on high in seeking to make the conditions of their life ennobling, not degrading. They were surely following a pillar of cloud and of fire in entering upon the quest of a life worthy to be called human. Had they not a right then to expect the aid of Him who encouraged this moral venture? Moses believed they had, and he cried unceasingly to the shuddering host: "Fear not; stand still and see the salvation of God; the Lord shall fight for you, and ye shall hold your peace."

Then above the roar of the storm, for the narrator tells us "a strong east wind" blew all night long, and above the tumult of the frightened people, there sounded the voice of the Great Ally: "Speak to the children of Israel, that they go forward." It seemed like a command to do the impossible. It was apparently the suggestion of an unattainable ideal. Here they were hemmed in on every side; on the right hand and the left there stretched the sand-hills of the desert where flight would have been useless; behind them came the horses and chariots of Pharaoh's army, driving furiously, and before them lay the arm of the Red Sea. Yet the divine command was: "Speak to the children of Israel, that they go forward," apparently mocking the peril and difficulty of their situation!

Futile as it seemed, however, at the call of their

leader they broke camp; the line of march was formed, the leaders were faced toward the sea, and the word was " Forward! " Then the strong east wind blew back the waters of that arm of the sea until it was shallow enough for them to cross. Into the bed of the sea they marched, and there, amid the roar of the wind and the flying foam—for, as Paul tells us, " they were all baptized unto Moses in the cloud and in the sea "—they went steadily forward by the divine command!

Before daybreak the Israelites were all safely across, but the Egyptians had come up during the night-watch, driving wearily and heavily across the wet sea-floor, their heavy chariot wheels clogged with the mud. And then suddenly the fierce wind veered about and the waters, scurrying before the blast, returned to their place, and the whole detachment of Pharaoh's army was drowned in the sea before it could escape.

It is a splendid poetic treatment of this incident which our author gives us. The strong east wind is God's chosen instrument, even as all the natural agencies are in Hebrew thought the servants of the divine will. " The winds and the waves, are they not all ministering spirits, sent forth to minister to the heirs of salvation? " The hailstones beating in the faces of the enemy, making possible for the

Hebrews that victory over his army, are tangible evidence that " the stars in their courses fight against Sisera." " Your Heavenly Father feeds the ravens and clothes the lilies," said Jesus, yet it is all done through the abiding natural order, with never a hint of any miracle wrought on behalf of bird or flower. It was the Hebrew habit of mind to see the hand and purpose of the God of their Fathers in all these natural phenomena. So here the strong east wind, which caused the waters to go back, making a pathway for the fleeing Israelites, and the subsequent shifting of the wind causing the waters to return and engulf the pursuing Egyptians, was to the narrator a direct manifestation of the divine intervention on behalf of the people He had undertaken to deliver.

And when those ancient Israelites thus witnessed the overthrow of their late oppressors, they stood upon the shore and sang to Him their song of triumph:

> The Lord is a man of war, Jehovah is His name!
> Pharaoh's chariots and his hosts hath He cast into the sea;
> The depths have covered them;
> They sank to the bottom as a stone.
> Thou didst blow with thy wind, the sea covered them.
> Thy right hand is become glorious in power.
> The Lord shall reign for ever and ever.

The Israelites were now on the road to industrial freedom; they were in the actual enjoyment of an opportunity to learn new lessons through the sense of responsibility. They were destined in the future to make sad blunders and to sin against the divine purpose, to fare scantily at times and to suffer pain; but in it all and through it all they would nevertheless learn and grow. The possession of freedom, with all the serious obligations it brought with it, would in time become their salvation.

The claim has been made repeatedly, and no doubt with some truth, that the colored race in our own Southern States was better fed, better clothed, better housed, and had on the whole a happier and more contented existence under slavery than it has had during the first forty years of its freedom. The master who said to an aspiring slave who was clamoring for his liberty, " You niggers have an easier time than I do," was well within the facts. And so was the ambitious slave who instantly retorted, " Yes, sah, and so does yo' hogs." The negro by his effective retort really anticipated the classical statement of John Stuart Mill: " It is better to be a dissatisfied man than a satisfied pig." Liberty has meant uncertainty, anxiety, obligation, which the colored people have not always known how to bear; but liberty has meant also a real education through the responsibility of self-control, and this has been worth all the pain it brought.

Wage-earners through their unions are insisting to-day upon a larger measure of liberty for themselves: they are urging their right to be heard in the determination of matters which were once left entirely to the decision of their employers. They are insisting on a more democratic spirit in the management of business, as to the wage-scale, the hours of labor, the conditions of employment, and the mode of payment. They suffer sometimes in these ventures; they make blunders and sin against economic and moral law in their initial efforts. But it is altogether right and best that they should be making the efforts—it will mean the coming at last of a much higher type of wage-earner. The effort for social betterment and the decision as to the various steps to be taken can never be made for the toilers by those who esteem themselves more competent— they must be made by the toilers themselves, to the end that the desired adequacy to the demands which improved conditions will inevitably bring may be gained through this responsible experience. All this Moses, the leader of this ancient movement, well knew, and he matriculated these untaught disciples of a better order in the school of responsible experience that night when he led them out of Egypt into the uncertain life of freedom in the peninsula of Sinai.

The whole event is so striking in its symbolism that the poet, the prophet, and the composer have in turn carried its details over and made them to represent crises in the spiritual life of the race. Here and there in the unfolding moral history of the world the souls of men have fled from conditions which seemed intolerable, only to find themselves confronted by still harder necessities. And when they seemed utterly shut in and driven to the point where there was no escape, their very helplessness and desperation led them to look up with new faith. Then somehow a way was opened for them in the midst of the deep. Up out of such situations of sorrow and adversity have come many of the best lives the world has ever known. Whole classes of people and entire nations have, in similar fashion, found themselves impeded in their true progress by obstacles apparently insurmountable, but thrown back upon their faith in God, by the very stress of a desperate situation, they have, under His wise guidance, discovered unexpected lines of advance.

We are at this very moment, in the social problems which confront us, hemmed in by obstacles which seem all but insurmountable; we have ahead of us a Red Sea standing in the way of an advance

toward that social amelioration pictured to us by
·the prophets of the hour. It is deep, wide, and
bank-full of problems and difficulties. It will require more than an all-night east wind to make a
way through it. On the right hand there is the
greed of many employers who want a lion's share
of the general product, that they may live in a useless and oftentimes hurtful luxury. On the left
hand there is the greed of many misguided wage-
earners who clamor for more than is consistent with
a successful continuance of the business. And driving furiously from behind, there are the horses and
chariots of a bargain-hunting public, wishing to buy
goods in abundance at prices lower than they can
be produced for under wholesome and equitable conditions!

Under all this combined pressure our poor industrial life seems driven at times to the point where
there is no escape. The longed-for deliverance cannot be secured in a single night by some one resolute
and fortunate movement—it can only come by years
of patient and far-seeing effort, as serious, aspiring
people shall follow where the pillar of cloud and of
fire points the way. But a race of men who had
brains enough and energy enough to develop here
in these United States an industrial organization unmatched for rapid, effective production, unequalled

thus far for the swift increase of the total wealth, surely can, if it will, accomplish still more. Men can use that same degree of energy and intelligence, together with a larger share of conscience, now made sensitive by the new sense of social responsibility, in the gradual development of an industrial organization in whose great rewards the poor and the helpless as well as the strong and the fortunate shall more equitably share. And to them at this hour the divine voice is speaking out of the darkness and the cloud, saying: " Speak to the children of America, that they go forward into a more justly administered, economic life."

CHAPTER VI

THE TRAINING IN INDUSTRIAL FREEDOM

WHEN the Israelites crossed the Red Sea, leaving behind them the fertile fields of the Nile delta, there stretched before them at once " the great and terrible wilderness." Instantly the food problem arose, and it necessarily became in the minds of the people of primary importance. The keen, dry air of the steppes and the long marches which their leader deemed expedient until they had left Egypt farther behind quickened their appetites until the visible food supply seemed altogether inadequate for the needs of such a multitude; and presently there was a great outcry against an expedition so hazardous, apparently, by reason of the slender resources of its commissary department. " Would God we had died by the hand of the Lord among the flesh-pots of Egypt," they cried to their leader. " You have brought us forth into the wilderness to kill us all with hunger." And thus the bread-and butter problem, which is always to the fore in any labor movement, became at once a matter of vital concern.

At this juncture they began to eat a certain sub-stance called " manna." We are told that it fell during the night with the dew, or gathered in tiny deposits like hoar frost on the shrubs of the desert. The people gathered it eagerly; they ground it in their rude mills and beat it in their mortars, making a coarse sort of cake. The Bedouins of to-day in that country make use of a food which they call " Mann es Sama," gathering it from the shrubs of that wild region, which may possibly sustain some relation to the food supply of those ancient Israel-ites. It is altogether unwise for any one to attempt to dogmatize upon these points, because it is not always easy to draw a hard-and-fast line between the prose and the poetry in some of these earlier narratives.

This manna was not their only source of suste-nance. We read also of their killing quails in great numbers; of their killing the cattle they had brought with them and boiling the flesh—when they set out from Egypt, " a mixed multitude went up also with them, and flocks and herds, even very much cattle." We are told of a bread made from wheat and barley which was obtained from the people of Seir; and of " cakes made from flour with oil." The rugged people of that region commonly subsist on the most meagre fare; and that the Israelites were not by any means well fed is evidenced by their murmuring desire to abandon the food supply derived from the manna and other sources and return to " the leeks and onions, the melons and cucumbers, in the land of Egypt," even though such a course would involve also a return to slavery. By these various means, however, they were kept alive during the hard period of their training.

The account of the administration of this food supply indicates that it was distributed among the people in an exceedingly democratic way. " They gathered each man according to his eating," the narrator says. Everybody worked; there was no leisure class, living idly and uselessly upon the labor of others. There was no unfair monopoly of the gifts of God's bounty by the strong to the detriment of the weak. They gathered each man according to his eating, each one consuming according to the actual service rendered, and not, as is often the case, those who consume the most doing, perhaps, the least in the work of actual production. The very principle upon which distribution was made, as stated by the narrator, sounds the note of an equitably organized industrial system—it is not entirely unlike the well-known motto of some of the modern socialists, " From each according to his powers, to each according to his needs."

The economic principle which entered into the administration of this ancient food supply has a legitimate bearing upon the present problem of distribution. Manna is not the only commodity which a benevolent Creator has given to the world to be administered on the general principle that "each man shall gather according to his eating." It is surely the divine intention that the land and the mines, the forests and the water-power, shall all be administered, not in the interest of the privileged few, but for the good of the producing many. Honest men may differ in judgment as to the best method for securing the realization of this high ideal, but the ideal itself seems imperative. The main justification for the private ownership of land lies in the necessity which exists for the application of individual labor to the land before it can possess any utility. In order to secure this persistent application of individual effort, it is necessary to have some system which will insure that desired result; and the main impression to be gained from human experience thus far is that private ownership of land is more fruitful in inducing the necessary individual effort than any other method thus far discovered of holding the soil.

But although this economic method may stand as the best means we have found thus far of attaining the end named, the privilege of private ownership ought to be so held within the firm grip of certain ethical principles as to make it socially helpful and not socially hurtful. When forceful and far-seeing individuals, or, still more forceful and far-seeing corporations, extend their holdings in such a way as to create an unnatural and injurious monopoly of these common resources, then the moral justification of that form of private ownership is destroyed and the fact stands plain that the bounty of the Creator is being used selfishly and wickedly. It is one of the heavy tasks resting to-day upon the awakened social conscience and the more thorough understanding of economic science, acting together, to discover some better methods of administering these great values created and intended for the general good.

When we set the present organization of society and the current methods of distribution in the searching presence of the commanding ideals held before us in the teaching of Christ, we are sore amazed over our failure to fulfil the divine purpose. We may well "tremble when we remember that God is just," in the face of all the glaring inequalities of condition among us, in the presence of the selfish monopolies bearing heavily upon the burdened and helpless poor. One multi-millionaire in New York has had so much to eat for decades past that he suffers continually from chronic indigestion and has, it is currently reported, a standing offer of one hundred thousand dollars to any physician who will give him once more a sound stomach. While at the same hour the charity boards inform us that in London alone there are eight hundred thousand people who never have enough to eat; that many of them, in order to check the cravings of hunger, go along the streets picking up the plum- and peach-stones which are dropped, that they may crack them and eat the pits; that they go also to the garbage-barrels and sort out that which is not too nauseating for them to be able to swallow in order to satisfy the gnawing hunger within.

Are we not forced to the conclusion that we have blundered and sinned, if those two glaring contrasts —the many over-fed millionaires suffering from chronic indigestion, weakened by their own luxury, the wholesome development of their children imperilled by the very abundance of material goods, on one side, and on the other the half a million poor people in a single city pouncing upon refuse and garbage to ward off starvation—are still so much in evidence? Has not our twentieth-century adminis-tration of the heavenly manna of God's bounty been unjust? We shall never have either industrial or spiritual peace, I am sure, until the relations of men are such that these contrasts in condition cease to be so inordinately cruel; until all the able-bodied people shall perform some useful labor — shall " gather according to their eating," thus rendering some genuine service to society proportioned to the share of goods which they appropriate for their personal enjoyment—instead of living, as many of them now do, upon the labor of others; until all the industrious children of men shall have more direct access to these common resources, to the end that they, too, may have the chance at least to gather each one according to his eating!

Absolute equality in outward condition is probably impossible so long as it pleases the Creator to divide ability so unequally, giving to one man ten talents, to another five, to another one; nor am I at all sure that absolute equality is desirable. " The effort of Jesus," as some one said recently, " was not to level down outward conditions, so much as to level up social ideals." But a more equitable distribution of the comforts of life and a more righteous administration of the common resources are plainly imperative if we are ever to stand right before Him who is no respecter of persons. And this can only be achieved through a more resolute and thorough-going application of intelligence and conscience to this vexed problem.

The strength of our best life must learn to say regarding the manifold resources now being so largely exploited for private gain, "This is the bread which the Lord our God has given us to eat." We must learn so to gather it and so to distribute it that those who by their strength gather much shall have nothing to waste in useless luxury, and those who in their weakness gather little shall have no lack. And in this noble endeavor we shall be instructed, I am confident, by turning ever and anon to these well-worn pages, and reading again the story of those ancient Israelites who, in the enjoyment of their manna, gained a new sense of their dependence upon God, and who, in their method of administering it, developed a new spirit of genuine consideration for the needs of all their fellows. The social renewal of any people is a long, slow process, and the years spent in gathering and eating the bread of the desert, even though the fare was sometimes meagre and the conditions of life severe, served to train them in a spirit profoundly useful for the days when they should enter perchance upon the possession of a richer abundance.

But there came a still more instructive and useful experience when the children of Israel approached the foot of Mount Sinai. They had gained their liberty and were breathing the free air of the steppes, their daily bread was within reach, by the gracious providence of God, but they had still to learn that neither men nor movements live by bread alone—they must live by every word which proceedeth out of the mouth of God. They must live by the sense of personal obligation and by the maintenance of spiritual fellowship with the Unseen; they must live by all the words of promise and command which issue from the mouth of the Most High! These ancient Israelites were there brought to realize that they must live by those great words which were thundered forth from the top of Sinai, touching the sacredness of life and purity, of truth and property, of family ties and religious obligations! Every movement for human betterment, if it is to result in any real and permanent advance, must come to the place where it feels the undisputed reign of law and the strong grip of moral obligation. It was imperative, therefore, that these children of Israel should in the early stages of their social undertaking bring their labor movement and pitch its camp beneath the shadow of Sinai.

The natural features of the region all tended to increase the religious suggestiveness of the situation in which they found themselves. Up out of a bare, rugged plain rose this mount of God like a huge, natural altar. Black clouds were seen to rest upon its top, as if some heavenly visitant had come down, veiling His glory in the thick darkness. Those Israelites who had lived all their lives in the flat delta of the Nile were profoundly impressed by the very sight of such a mountain! They instinctively began to lift up their eyes unto the hills from whence should come help!

It is also a region of terrific storms—the wind roars through the rocks like the blast of a trumpet; the fierce glare of the lightning and the crash of thunder give the impression of supernatural power. All these phenomena are frankly interpreted in the narrative as evidence of the presence and power of the deity, who had taken those untutored Israelites in charge. The roar of the wind was the loud blast of His trumpet, summoning them before Him; the fierce glare of the lightning was a momentary glimpse of that divine glory which no man could see and live; the peal of the thunder was as the sound of a divine voice calling upon the people for obedience. We can readily understand how all these phenomena might naturally fill the hearts of uninstructed slaves, hitherto unaccustomed to either mountains or storms, with a profound sense of mystery and awe!

The narrative states clearly that it did make a

deep impression upon their primitive minds. Moses had told them in Egypt that Yahweh, the God of their ancestors—Abraham, Isaac, and Jacob—had appeared to him at the foot of this mountain, declaring His interest in the oppressed children of Israel, and announcing His purpose to deliver them. This same Yahweh had sent a message by the hand of Moses to Pharaoh demanding their release. When the monarch refused, Yahweh had smitten all his borders with plague and pestilence. This Yahweh had then brought the Israelites safely through the Red Sea; He had fed them with manna on the way; and now they were actually encamped at the foot of Sinai, which was to them as His earthly residence. They were ready and expectant, therefore, awaiting further instruction at His hands.

On a certain day the eyes of all the waiting people were fixed upon the top of the sacred mount. Would Yahweh, their God, appear to them, they wondered, in any visible form? Would He stand before them as a winged figure, like the gods of the Assyrians, or as a huge bull, like the gods of Egypt? The awful storm was at its height, for " it came to pass," the narrator says, " on the third day there was a thick cloud upon the top of the mount, and there were lightnings and thunder and the sound of a trumpet." All these phenomena were to their untutored minds direct manifestations of the Presence of the mysterious and powerful Being who was there to reveal Himself to them from the top of the mount. The minds of all the multitude were keenly alive, eagerly anticipating the appearance of some celestial being.

But when Moses, their representative, had gone to the top of the mount to meet this deity, and had returned, neither he nor they had seen any shape or form. Moses came back simply bearing in his hands the elements of the moral law. He assured them that the God of their fathers revealed Himself to men most of all in those ideas and principles which have to do with right conduct; that He spoke to them in commandments regarding the divine insistence upon the sacredness of life and purity, of truth and property, of family ties and religious obligations —and this is what the people there saw as divine when they encamped before Sinai! Down through all the years of their growth this continued to be the main element in their thought of God—He was a God of righteousness, to whom it were vain and irreverent to attempt to assign any definite form; He was a God who was to be honored chiefly by loving obedience to His moral commands. And in that far-distant time when the holy ark of the covenant was opened, " there was nothing therein," we read

—no image, no sacred utensils, no tools of magic—
"nothing save the two tables of the law, which
Moses placed therein at Horeb!"

There are three accounts of those ten commandments given in the Scriptures—one in the thirty-
fourth chapter of Exodus, one in the twentieth
chapter of Exodus, and one in the fifth chapter of
Deuteronomy. It is probable that the lower and
cruder form, as contained in the thirty-fourth chapter
of Exodus, came first, and that the nobler form of
these precepts came later, through the moral growth
of the people and the fuller disclosure which God
made of Himself as their spiritual vision cleared.
But the foundations at least of this divine law were
laid in those early days, and it is interesting to see
now to what useful expression they have finally
come in the ordinarily accepted "Ten Commandments."

The great background of the whole code lay in the
fact that the God of the Hebrews was one God—
He had no divine associates, no relatives. There
never was a Hebrew goddess; and this fact alone
saved their religion from a world of unwholesome
theory and practice into which other early religions
so readily fell. God is one—"I AM, hath sent me
unto you." "I am the Lord thy God that brought
thee up out of the land of Egypt, out of the house

of bondage. Thou shalt have no other gods before me!"

Then, guarding the sacredness of that faith in one
God, at a time when religion so easily became mean
and vile, this ancient code declared that idolatry is
wrong—" Thou shalt not make any graven image ";
irreverence is wrong—" Thou shalt not take the
name of the Lord thy God in vain "; religious indifference is wrong—" Remember the Sabbath day to
keep it holy." This constantly recurring holy day
would tend to keep alive in the hearts of the people
a sense of the legitimate claim which Jehovah their
God had upon them. Thus these first commandments carefully guarded the sacredness of that
faith in one God, by their stern prohibition of those
sins which would most readily weaken or destroy it.

Then straight on into the fundamental human relations these commandments went. Family ties are
sacred—" Honor thy father and thy mother." Human life is sacred—" Thou shalt not kill." Purity
between the sexes is sacred—" Thou shalt not commit adultery." Property is sacred—" Thou shalt
not steal." Truth is sacred—" Thou shalt not bear
false witness." All the interests of others are sacred
—" Thou shalt not covet anything that is thy neighbor's." Simple and elementary these injunctions
are, but at a time when other religions, with their

gods many and their lords many, with their unwholesome traditions about wayward goddesses and
their utterly debasing stories of celestial escapades,
were full of untruth and uncleanness; at a time when
disregard for life and purity, for truth and property, made moral progress difficult, these early commandments shine with a wondrous splendor! They
stand, indeed, as the genuine expression of a moral
order, august, cosmic, eternal, under whose beneficent rule all men and all movements must at last
be brought if they are ever to reach the land of
promise.

When we turn to the industrial agitation in modern times we find a growing tendency to recognize
this plain truth. John Mitchell, in the great coal
strike of 1902, used to say constantly to the miners
of Pennsylvania, by spoken address and through the
columns of the press, " Refrain from law-breaking!
If you want to spoil your own cause and lose every
sacrifice you have made for yourselves and your
families, give way to your temper and commit some
violence. Lawlessness and violence will alienate
public sympathy and lose our cause, as indeed they
ought." And he has said the same thing, over and
over, in his book on " Organized Labor," which
every minister of the Gospel ought to read. And
what is all this but simply a far-off echo of what

God said in that ancient labor movement three thousand years ago—" Thou shalt not kill, nor steal, nor in any wise destroy! "

It is manifestly wrong for union men to break the wrists of other men or to resort to any sort of violence to prevent their working during a strike. It is also manifestly wrong for men to attempt to break down by unfair methods the human standard of living, which is more precious even than wrists. It matters not whether the wrong to another's life is done in a moment of violence, or done slowly by measures which mean the degradation of the essential elements of human life—" Thou shalt not in any wise kill, nor steal, nor destroy! " In every labor union and in every employers' association, in all the agitation of the hour and in all the plans for industrial betterment, Mount Sinai must forever stand before the eyes of men with its solemn warnings and august sanctions, with its imperative " Thou shalt " and " Thou shalt not! "

I emphasize this point because in much of the industrial agitation there is a disposition to ignore those chains which ignorance and incapacity, idleness and intemperance, fasten upon the wrists of great numbers of unhappy men. Emancipation for such individuals cannot be accomplished by change in the industrial organization unaided by this new

sense of relationship to that moral order which
Mount Sinai symbolized. I emphasize it also because there is a tendency on the part of the well-
to-do to forget the sacredness which should attach
to life and purity, to truth and property, to home
ties and religious obligations among those humble
toilers whose personal and family interests are to-
day so largely at the mercy of those who employ
them.

The memory of those days at Sinai never altogether faded out of the minds of these ancient Hebrews. They made their blunders, they were guilty
of wrong-doing, for they were men and not angels;
but through all the succeeding years there was the
growing feeling that the main office of religion was
not to confer personal advantage, either present or
prospective, but rather to induce and enable men
to do right in all their dealings with their fellows
and in the way they bore themselves toward their
Maker. This idea that God is pleased with righteousness, and with nothing else, was by no means
common in those early days—and it is not even now
so universal in the religious thinking of the world
as to be entirely commonplace. The rude stone tab-
lets on which they chiselled these divine commands
—so simple at first that they were habitually called
" the ten words "—were kept in a place of honor in

the ark of the covenant; they were carried along by the people in all their wilderness wanderings; and on the first approach to the land of promise, they were borne by the priests at the head of the marching host, fit symbols of that moral order to which they looked for wholesome guidance.

In that sign they conquered; and in that sign only can men conquer now. We may ask if we choose in regard to any industrial arrangement, "Is it expedient?" "Is it shrewd?" "Will it win?" But no genuine progress will be made until we come to ask steadily and sternly in regard to our whole course of action and our prevailing method in these matters, "Is it right?" All methods which are morally wrong have against them the God of Abraham and of Isaac and of Jacob, the God of Israel, and of Egypt and of America; and in time He will relentlessly beat down all those wrong methods into the dust. And, conversely, all wise and just efforts which have as their object the deliverance of the people from industrial oppression and social wrong have this same God powerfully on their side; and though for forty years and more they wander in the desert of failure and experiment, they will come at last, under His sure guidance, into full possession of the land of promise.

These commandments of old were not all prohibi-

tions, nor were they the mere commonplaces of mo-
rality. How much it means that there in the very
heart of them, printed as they are in our holy books,
inscribed on the walls of our churches, chanted by
our choirs in public worship, there stands an act to
regulate the hours of labor! That fourth command-
ment was meant to secure for all the weary toilers
of earth one rest day in every seven—alas, that human greed and hard necessity have so often robbed
the weary of their birthright! It was clearly an
instance of labor legislation. So far as history records, the first attempt ever made to regulate the
hours of labor by law was made there at Sinai,
when the Lord God spoke to a company of working-
men just delivered from bondage, and said, " Six
days shalt thou labor and do all thy work, but the
seventh day is the Sabbath of the Lord thy God : in it
thou shalt not do any work, thou nor thy son, nor
thy daughter, nor thy man-servant, nor thy maid-
servant, nor thine ox, nor thine ass, nor any of thy
cattle, nor thy stranger that is within thy gates, that
thy man-servant and thy maid-servant may rest as
well as thou. And thou shalt remember that thou
wast a servant in the land of Egypt. And that the
Lord thy God brought thee out thence through a
mighty hand and by an outstretched arm; therefore
the Lord thy God commanded thee to keep the Sab-

bath day." They were urged to keep this rest day, for themselves and for their employés, in grateful remembrance of the fact that the Author of the command had delivered them from Egypt, where they once toiled unceasingly without the blessed truce of one rest day in seven. In view of this divine utterance regulating the hours of labor, all those critics who feel that the discussion of industrial problems before the altars of religion is somewhat out of place might do well to read once more the Ten Commandments, as they stand recorded in the fifth chapter of Deuteronomy.

Other items of industrial legislation attributed by the narrator to a divine source during this period will occur to every one. Usury was forbidden. Personal clothing or the necessary tools of a man's trade were not to be seized for debt. Wages were not to be retained when due, to the embarrassment of those who had earned them. The pawn shops, which apparently had already appeared among the Hebrews, were not to keep overnight a heavy garment which had been pledged—the debtor was to be allowed the comfort of it during the hours of sleep. Just weights, a just hin, and a just balance were made mandatory by divine edict. Rigorous commands were given against all manner of bribery. Painstaking sanitary provisions were laid down, for ritualistic rather than for hygienic reasons it may have been at first, but vindicating themselves in the improved health of the people. Directions as to the treatment of leprosy, abscesses, and the fumigation of houses in case of contagious illness all issued from Jehovah.

The doctrine of land attributed to Moses is of the greatest industrial significance—it provided for titles to be held in such a way that land could not be permanently alienated from the family line or monopolized for any length of time by the strong to the injury of the weak. The poor were also provided for in a way that would go far toward preserving both their self-respect and the habit of industry—the vines were not to be entirely stripped of grapes, nor the olive-trees beaten a second time, nor the corners of the wheat fields reaped. Something was to be left in all these quarters for the poor, and these provisions made it possible for the needy to thus gain assistance at the expenditure of a certain effort on their own behalf. These are but a few of the many social and industrial questions dealt with in the legislation of that day. They make plain the fact that the ideal before the minds of the leaders of the movement was a fraternal community under the paternal care of God, who was literally the head of that theocratic system. Their thought was that the divine wisdom addressed itself frankly and thoroughly to the task of establishing for all the oppressed a new social order, which would in its very terms be calculated to encourage spiritual progress.

Here under the shadow of Sinai, then, those Israelites were made to feel that all high privileges are accompanied by serious obligations. In the full enjoyment of their new-found freedom they immediately discovered that there was laid upon them a holy responsibility touching the use to be made of those advantages—even as the man who insists to-day upon his right to manage his own business in his own way should be made to realize that such right is modified by his obligation to manage it in such a way that his prosperity shall include a fair measure of prosperity for the men whose interests and destinies are bound up with his own in that enterprise. And the man who insists upon his right to work, at anything he pleases and for anything he pleases, should remember that that right is modified by his obligation not to imperil human standards of living for the whole class of men with whom he stands. The moral bearing of our acts upon the interests of others must be considered always, even more than our own present and personal advantage. The word of God from Sinai, touching the moral obligations which accompany all material advantages, must be heard and heeded. 'Ye have seen what I did unto the Egyptians, because of you. Now, therefore, obey my voice and keep my covenant, and ye shall be a treasure unto me above all people. Keep these words, and do them, that it may be well with thee in the land which the Lord thy God giveth thee.'

But straight in the face of their open vision of this moral order, and of the divine favor which would rest upon them if they observed it, there came a disgraceful falling away. It is painful always to see a man or a movement faced right but " staining the even virtue of its enterprise " by moral fault, and it is painful here to turn the leaf and read the next chapter in the story of this ancient labor movement. In the absence again of competent leadership, " when the people saw that Moses delayed to come down out of the mount," they gathered themselves to Aaron, saying, " Up, make us gods to go before us; as for this Moses, the man who brought us up out of the land of Egypt, we wot not what is become of him." The absence of some one whose wisdom and character would enable him to point the way in such fashion that the people would be ready to follow, became the immediate occasion of their downfall.

Jehovah was indeed their God and their Guide, but He was unseen. In the thoughts of many of those uninstructed slaves He was far away. They craved some visible, tangible embodiment of that supreme leadership. God in the skies, or Moses, His prophet, at the top of the sacred mount, ceased to influence them—they demanded a leader who mingled daily in the life of the camp. It is the face like our own face, looking upon us with divine compassion, the hand like our own hand, pointing the way, and the heart like ours, tempted in all points as we are, and thus possessed of genuine sympathy, which bring that assurance of the divine interest that becomes effective. The foolish idolatry of those early Israelites when they said to Aaron, " Up, make us gods," was a misdirected and disastrous attempt to bring God near, but it sprang from that same need of an ever-present leadership, divine in spirit, but human and visible in its real manifestation.

And is not that, I repeat again, the sorest need of the toiling and burdened children of America to-day? The leadership they really crave, in order to be genuinely effective, must, in my judgment, follow the main lines of the method of the Incarnation. It must needs be born in lowly conditions, in the manger of a stable perhaps in some Bethlehem of Judea. It must know the plain fare, the daily toil, the humble surroundings, and make its increase in stature, in wisdom, and in grace through the experience of some useful trade, like that of the carpenter. It must, for a complete realization of the wide-spread anxiety touching the means of support, have known days when it had not where to lay its head. It must be able to announce its mission, with the genuine note of reality, in some such words as these: " The Spirit of the Lord is upon me, because he hath anointed me to preach good tidings to the poor; he hath sent me to bind up the broken-hearted, to preach deliverance to the captives, and to set at liberty them that are bruised." It may, indeed, in the fulfilment of its mission, be compelled to lay down its life for the sheep, and possibly to die outside the gates, unblessed by the ecclesiasticism of its day—such has been the fate of some of the noblest examples of moral leadership the world has ever seen, and the painful story may not be even yet complete. The general type of leadership which is to advance the interests of the laboring people of America is certainly indicated in broad outlines by the life of the Carpenter of Nazareth. The One who was able to make the high claim, " I am the way," took not on Him " the nature of angels—He took the seed of Abraham," the nature of His own

race: " He took upon himself the form of a servant," and went about doing good; He became
humbly obedient to all the demands of an exacting
service.

An angel of economic wisdom sitting comfortably
apart in a well-endowed university chair, or an arch-
angel of piety standing up in a well-supported, well-
guarded pulpit, lecturing the humble toilers on their
shortcomings, will never suffice. Some one who has
himself done rough work, earned his bread by the
sweat of his brow, kept warm his sympathies with
the wage-earning millions by actually sharing their
lot, yet who is withal wise and just, must come to
state the message of God to his fellows in the language in which they were born, and to point the
way by walking in it on his own two feet. That type
of leadership, I believe, is the most pressing need
in the industrial struggle to-day; and for lack of it,
many people still go off after false gods and degrade
their high contention by the debasing idolatry of
force.

In response to the request of those mistaken Israelites, Aaron took their ornaments of gold and
fashioned for them a golden calf. The form of the
idol was naturally determined by the influence of
an earlier environment. In Egypt they had witnessed the worship of the sacred bull Apis with all

the stately ritual of that ancient cult. Aaron therefore set up this golden calf and made proclamation:
" These be thy gods, O Israel, which brought thee
up." The Israelites in the Nile delta had seen the
ruling and successful classes, under whose power
they had toiled, worshipping the sacred bulls, and
the power of that example was still strong upon
them. They sang and danced before the golden calf
in the ardor of religious feeling; they cast aside their
loose garments, dancing half-naked in unseemly ex-
citement, like the dervishes of the East, before this
god of gold; they also prostrated themselves before
it in reverent allegiance. It was a horrible and a
saddening sight that met the eye of Moses as he
came down the side of the mount!

But there was nothing surprising in it all—bull-
worship was a leading feature in the devotion of
the most successful people those Israelites had ever
known. Let similar cause exist anywhere, and a
similar result will follow inevitably. Let the well-
to-do people of any nation in any period of the
world's history preach, for example, the gospel of
materialism; let them say by their actions (which
speak louder than prayers) that big dinners and
fine clothing, palatial homes and costly entertainments, expensive yachts and high-priced automobiles,
are the main things in life! let them say, " These

be the gods which bring us up into happiness and peace "—and slowly but surely the toiling people will also be materialized. And this passion for material advantage may become so strong as to impel the plain people to lawless and cruel efforts in order to gain some of these joys for themselves. Let the gods of gold be set up by the leaders of society in the place of intelligence and aspiration, in the place of high moral purpose and the spirit of social service, and presently a large part of the nation will be prostrated in a degrading worship of material success.

Materialism as a philosophical system is in a bad way—many of our wisest men are saying that it is actually on its last legs. The main drift of the best science and of the best philosophy of the hour is toward the claim that final reality is not matter, but mind or spirit. Those men who noisily proclaim that " there is nothing in human nature which cannot be accounted for by chemistry," and that " vice and virtue are as purely the products of physical forces as sugar and vitriol," are merely belated minds overtaken by darkness, and shouting to keep up their courage. The men who can see the horse but cannot see the rider who guides him are being convicted to-day, by a more searching diagnosis, as afflicted with intellectual astigmatism. Materialism as a philosophical system, therefore, does not now

cut much figure in the world of careful thought.
But materialism as a moral tendency, in shaping
ideals and in determining lines of action, is dread-
fully and wickedly active and powerful. " These
be thy gods," men cry, touching those things which
can be bought for gold and sold again for more gold
—" These be the gods which bring us up to happiness and peace! " Yet the whole ugly claim is as
false and as disastrous as was the word of Aaron
there in the wilderness of Sinai!

" Comfort first and character afterward," is the
mistaken order proposed by these modern idolaters.
Seek first all the good things of this world, and
then, when you have them, you will be in a comfortable condition to give thought to the kingdom
of God and His righteousness—this is the unnatural
order actually proposed by certain social reformers
to the wage-earners. But the order is altogether
wrong, as you see when you look into the hearts
and into the histories of those families who have
steadily put comfort first and character afterward.
Physical wants are not the wants which take precedence over all others. The method of Him who
said " Thy sins be forgiven thee " before He said
" Arise and walk " is the philosophical method.
Seek first reverence, trust, and obedience toward
Him whose great aid you need in your effort; seek

the spirit of justice, truth, and purity toward your fellow-men, and then you will be in a position steadily to add all those things which make for abundant and joyous life! This is thy God, O Israel, and not those shameful substitutes which are wickedly put forward in His place!

Moses came down the mountainside, his eyes resting upon the ugly idolatry, his heart heavy with discouragement over the fickleness of those favored people, and his whole attitude terrible in its righteous indignation! With blanched face Aaron entreated him: 'Let not the anger of my lord wax hot; thou knowest this people that they are set on evil. They said, 'Make us gods,' and I said, 'Whosoever hath any gold let him break it off and bring it to me.' And I cast it into the fire—and there came out this calf!' He disclaimed all responsibility in the matter, as do all weak-kneed sinners who would lay the entire blame for their own wrongdoing on some outside fact—the people wanted a god; he cast the gold into the fire, and the fire did the rest! But Moses sharply reprimanded him for his share in this moral lapse; he broke up the idol and burned it in the fire; he ground it to powder, strewing the dust upon water which he forced the people to drink. And no apology is needed for that expression of wrath, because hatred of evil, hot, live, and terrible, is simply the reverse side of the love of good! The milksop, incapable of such moral indignation, is not spiritually sound. The wrath of God Himself is a real and inevitable attribute of His perfect character, because indignation, terrible and eternal, against the evil which would ruin His children is absolutely imperative in a God of holy love.

Had Moses, in the spirit of easy toleration, acquiesced in the worship of the golden calf, the cry would have rung out, from day to day, " These be thy gods, O Israel," until the false claim would have come to be widely believed. The high moral purpose and the spiritual aspiration which characterized the movement at the outset would have faded out, and those Hebrews would have lapsed into a few wandering tribes worshipping the bull of brute force, or prostrating themselves before the material value of a golden idol. In the absence of any fundamental, commanding, and ever-enlarging allegiance, this ancient labor movement would have ended in dismal failure. It was imperative, therefore, that this people should be held firmly to the worship of the unseen God, who ever leads His people on and up through their growing devotion to the highest conception of the divine their minds can grasp.

And with no less moral determination and spiritual passion than was manifest in this action of

Moses, there must likewise come to our modern life a resolute calling away of the people from the unseemly idolatry of material success, a facing toward those spiritual ideals which alone insure permanent and thorough well-being. In the conversation of the home and in the spirit of social life, in the discussion of industrial problems and in the voice of literature, in the real aims of the university and in the teaching of the churches, there must come a profound turning away from slavish allegiance to the ambition for material accumulation. There must ring out a fresh summons to the definite worship of the living God.

If society fails at this point the very movements which have as their aim the betterment of men will die for want of moral energy. The spiritual impulse, which must lie at the heart of all the splendid efforts of mankind, would in such case be wanting, and the progress of the race would therefore be stayed. Monopoly, luxury, and moral indifference destroyed the Roman Empire because they set up idols for men's regard which were not meant to be the objects of their fundamental allegiance. And the unwholesome idolatry of an outward success, often unjustly and unworthily achieved in modern times, must give place to nobler aspirations in the market and in the polling-place, in the counting-room

and in the language of the press, in the ambitions
of the student and in the upward look of the wor-
shipper, if we, too, are not to meet with a similar
fate.

These three main lessons, then, the Israelites
learned in the days of their wandering through the
wilderness of Sinai: First, they learned that men live
in the last analysis by the bounty of God, and that
the best results are only gained when the food supplies are so equitably administered that each man
gathers according to his eating, the strong so consecrating their strength that they have nothing to
waste, and the weak so aided in their feebler effort
that they have no lack. Second, they learned that
the whole struggle for industrial, domestic, social,
and political well-being must be carried on under the
shadow of and in growing harmony with a moral
order, symbolized by the stern presence of Sinai,
visibly and audibly insistent upon the sacredness of
life and purity, of truth and property, of family ties
and religious obligations. And, finally, they learned
that there cannot safely be set up any symbol of
brute force or any gods of gold in the place of Him
who is entitled to receive the utmost devotion of our
hearts, and who alone is able to produce that quality
of life which shall gain entrance into the land of
promise.

CHAPTER VII

WE saw these Israelites, in the last lecture, brought immediately under the power of a divine law there at Mount Sinai. They were made to feel that in their struggle for industrial betterment they must adjust all their efforts to the moral order which enfolded them. They saw that this moral order was universal and abiding—they could no more escape from it than from the power of gravitation.

But the content of the law given at Sinai, made up, as it was, so largely of " Thou shalt nots," did not embody all that was essential for their moral unfolding. It did indeed guard the sacredness of life and purity, of truth and property, of family ties and of religious obligations, chiefly by throwing around them the high fence of certain prohibitions. It was necessary, however, that there should be in the hearts of these men that positive spirit of service and of devotion to the common good requisite for permanent progress in social well-being. We find, therefore, in the further narrative of their experiences, the demand made for a sacrificial life: "An altar shalt thou make, and offer thereon burnt offerings and peace offerings."

The whole history of the idea of sacrifice is a most interesting one. In the minds of many primitive peoples the consecration of any form of life to God was best accomplished by killing and burning it. They brought the firstlings of their flocks and slew them with religious ceremony. They laid the bodies of these slain beasts upon the altar and burned them. As the flames consumed the offering, taking it utterly out of their hands, as the smoke rose toward the sky and the fragrance of the roasted meat was wafted upward, the people truly believed that there was being carried into the very presence of the deity they worshipped the essence and sweet savor of their offering.

We find this primitive habit of thought manifesting itself sometimes even in the consecration of the lives of human beings. It was not unusual for fathers, in the extravagance and crudity of their desire to show devotion to their deities, to offer up their own children in sacrifice. Abraham the traditional father of the Hebrew people temporarily influenced on one occasion by this mistaken idea, took his son Isaac to Mount Moriah to offer him as a sacrifice to Jehovah, as if to indicate that his devotion to his

God was no less complete than the devotion of the people around him to their gods. And the offering of that son to God was, in his misguided judgment, to be best accomplished by killing and burning him with religious ceremony.

There was gradually emerging, however, under the tuition of the Divine Spirit, a nobler idea of sacrifice. Here and there certain moral leaders in Israel were coming to believe that they could give their offerings to God without burning and destroying them—that, indeed, it would be more acceptable in His sight to preserve them and use them for His service. We find this nobler conception of sacrifice drawn out clearly and at length by the prophets of the eighth century. And even to Abraham himself in that supreme hour on Mount Moriah, the author of the narrative says, there came the suggestion of this truer form of devotion. The impulse to give his son to Jehovah was of divine origin—it was " a word of the Lord " which came to him. The form, however, which the consecration of his son at first took in the father's purpose was a mistaken form suggested by the rude environment where human sacrifices were not uncommon. But there on the mount of sacrifice, under the open sky, when the father actually stretched out his hand to slay his own son, some final misgiving as to the righteousness of his course, some look of consternation and appeal on the face of the child, perhaps, some sober second thought as to whether any useful end would be served by such an act, came to this devoted patri- arch as the voice of God from heaven. His hand was stayed. He looked up and saw a ram caught in the bushes. He accepted that as a further indi- cation from on high that the life of his son should be spared. He joyously took the ram and offered it instead, keeping his son alive and consecrating him to God in more intelligent fashion by training him for a life of usefulness. And in the succeeding years this nobler conception of sacrifice, as best ac- complished by preserving and using the devoted object for the glory of God and the service of men, came to be gradually established in the minds of all the more intelligent worshippers.

The real value of these ancient sacrifices lay mainly in what they symbolized. The round and round of sacrifice and burnt offering, which to the careless reader seems so meaningless, aided in the development of that habit of mind which subordi- nates private interest to the larger good. The gift of the first-fruits and of the firstlings of the flock became the symbol of devotion to certain ideals which God held before the people. It was the an- ticipation of that worthier sacrifice which the people would make when once they learned to give themselves to unselfish service. Jesus the Messiah, the very crown and consummation of religious development among the Hebrews, brought no lamb or bullock to be slain at the altar, though such sacrifices were usual in His day. He brought Himself. The actual shedding of His own blood upon the cross was accomplished, not by Himself nor by His followers nor by the God whose will He came to do—it was accomplished by His bigoted and cruel enemies. The real offering and sacrifice was made by Christ Himself in the depths of His own spirit when, by the dedication of His own life to redemptive effort, " He gave Himself for us." This eternal readiness on His part to give His life a ransom for many was what the seer on Patmos called " The Lamb slain from the foundation of the world."

The same moral necessity for this spirit of sacrifice which existed when those Israelites threw off their slavery and began their struggle for freedom exists now. " An altar shalt thou make and sacrifice thereon! " If the busy, self-seeking world forgets or neglects this fundamental requirement, it does so at its peril. Wherever self-interest is followed solely, disaster will surely come. It matters not whether it be the self-interest of an association of capitalists intent solely upon their own gain because they hold a monopoly on certain goods; or the self-interest of a federation of labor unions forcing unreasonable demands because they hold a monopoly of the employable labor of the community; or the self-interest of the two acting together, as they have done in certain cities, making the helpless public pay heavy tribute through the unjust demands of those who have the consumers at their mercy—in either event such a selfish course brings disaster to those larger interests which ought to be held steadily in view. "An altar shalt thou make and sacrifice thereon," for in ways appropriate to modern conditions there must be to-day that same subordination of private interest to the general good!

We find a strong statement of this principle in a widely read utterance made at a notable meeting held some time ago in Faneuil Hall, Boston. The members of the Central Labor Council of that city invited President Eliot, of Harvard University, to address them. For an hour he spoke to them in the old "Cradle of Liberty" from a carefully written paper, and then, for more than an hour longer, he replied to questions from the floor asked by the labor-union men. Many words of truth and justice were spoken, as one would expect from the character and ability of the man; and, among the rest, these significant words regarding the spirit of class selfishness:

"The fundamental object of the Labor Union or of the employers' association," said President Eliot, "seems to be merely the pecuniary advantage of its class; and these organizations are exhibiting that same class selfishness which, in other centuries, has been exhibited by nobilities, priesthoods, and soldieries. The world has had bitter experience of the evils resulting from the class selfishness of these aristocratic, ecclesiastical, and military combinations; and democracy does well to distrust the new development of this class selfishness, however different the classes may be which now manifest these dangerous qualities."

All this was saying in modern language what God said to these Israelites thirty centuries ago. An altar shalt thou make, a habit of mind shalt thou build into the common life, where self-interest is subordinated to the larger good, where consecration and public spirit are exalted above private gain! The form of this devotion must necessarily be determined by surrounding conditions, but the call for genuine sacrifice is just as imperative to-day as when altars of burnt-offering were sending up their smoke from the hill-sides of Judea. This habit of mind and this quality of character cannot safely be left out of

any social system which is to abide for any length of time.

I am not for a moment supposing that this spirit is entirely wanting in modern life. It is because we have many men of public spirit, habitually seeking their personal welfare only as it is included in the general welfare, steadily administering large business interests in the spirit of genuine and intelligent good-will, that we enjoy such peace and security as we do possess. But there are, all about us, enemies of our peace who have by no means caught that spirit. They have never taken to heart that fundamental demand, " An altar shalt thou make and sacrifice thereon! "

Look around you at the scale of expenditure commonly practised by certain classes of people—many of them Christian people and members of our leading churches. It has increased in the last twenty-five years at a dizzying rate. Costly hotels and palatial yachts, ornament and luxury dazzling in their magnificence, gorgeous social entertainments which would have made kings rub their eyes a century ago —in all these ways money is being poured out in certain quarters like water!

The rate of interest on money is much lower than twenty-five years ago. Ordinary profits are smaller, we are told, and returns from investments narrower and more uncertain. Yet all the while certain classes of people are living more and more expensively, at the very time when, according to the official reports regarding poor relief in the great cities, the number of people to whom bread is a matter of constant anxiety steadily increases. It forces upon you the conviction that the great gulf between such luxury and such penury means a lack of equity in the distribution of the products of the world's common toil. When you travel, or enter the homes and the hotels and the pleasure-grounds of the well-to-do, you are amazed that there is so much money to be spent on luxury! When you walk with Jane Adams through Chicago, or with Jacob Riis through lower New York, or with Charles Booth through the East End of London, you are amazed again that so many people are living in penury! Does it not seem as if the warning of President Eliot regarding class selfishness was sorely needed by a vast number of people not represented in the Central Labor Council of Boston? That great word of God, " An altar shalt thou make," a spirit shalt thou show, which exalts the general good above private gain or personal indulgence, is still plainly required.

Let me refer again to a single symptom of our modern life—the amazing and disgraceful increase of child-labor in this land of opportunity! I quote the following figures from " The Social Unrest," by John Graham Brooks:

" From the year 1870 to 1880, among those employed in the cotton factories of the South, the number of men over sixteen years of age increased ninety-two per cent, the number of women over sixteen, seventy-seven per cent, and the number of children under sixteen, one hundred and forty per cent. The increase of child-labor was almost equal to the combined increase of the labor of adult men and women.

" From 1880 to 1890 the number of men over sixteen increased only twenty-one per cent, the number of women over sixteen increased two hundred and sixty-nine per cent, and the number of children increased one hundred and six per cent. The increase of the number of women and children employed in these mills was eighteen times as great as the entire increase of the number of men.

" From 1890 to 1900 the number of men over sixteen increased seventy-nine per cent, the number of women over sixteen, one hundred and fifty-eight per cent, and the number of children under sixteen, two hundred and seventy per cent. The increase of child-labor in the last decade was more than fifty per cent in excess of the total increase of adult labor."

According to the official report for 1890 from the Labor Bureau of North Carolina, the only State in the South presenting an official report upon labor statistics, less than ten per cent of the operatives in the textile-mills of that State were under fourteen years of age ten years ago, while, according to the report for 1901, those under fourteen now constitute nearly eighteen per cent of the whole number employed. Out of a total of forty-five thousand and forty-four textile operatives, seven thousand nine hundred and ninety-six, or almost one-fifth, are children under fourteen; and during that same period the average daily wage of the child has been decreased from thirty-two to twenty-nine cents per day.

More than twenty thousand children—a standing army of social menace in itself—are at work in these mills at the present moment. It is the opinion of some Southern investigators that, if the truth were told in each case, in place of the fictitious statements as to age offered by many unscrupulous parents, and all too readily accepted by some equally unscrupulous mill superintendents, it would be found that fully one-third of these twenty thousand children are under ten years of age. This certainly means a very heavy legacy of future inequalities to be faced and borne. These little children, working in the cotton-mills be-

fore they are ten years old—many of them working
on the night shift, and thus compelled to gain what
broken and troubled sleep they may during the
hours of daylight—will inevitably grow up with depleted vitality, and they will, as a consequence, go
to swell the number of deficients, delinquents, and
dependents in the various communities where they
dwell. This inhuman desire to increase profits by
utilizing the cheap labor of the child needs to be
brought face to face with that divine altar where
God demands that selfish gain be subordinated to
the larger interests at stake.

In the days of Robert Owen a certain manufacturer, who had pronounced legal interference with
child-labor "the maudlin sentimentalism of those
who know neither business nor human nature," was
compelled to admit under close examination that he
had been making in the business of cotton manufacture over two hundred per cent in yearly profits
on his actual investment. Yet he, and the group of
men who stood with him in opposing the regulation
of child-labor by law, maintained that they could
not afford to dispense with the labor of the children
because "that would drive the business out of England!" The Southern mills in our own country are
not making any such profit as that to-day, but some of
them have been making, according to their own pub-

lished statements, a very large per cent upon the capital actually invested, and they, too, are using the same argument, that they " cannot afford to do away with the child's help because of Northern competition."

And why are all these thousands of ten- and twelve-year-old children thrust into the mills to work eleven or twelve hours a day for an average wage of twenty-nine cents? Fathers and mothers in North Carolina, Alabama, and Georgia feel toward their children very much as other parents feel. But these parents are poor, and because their own wages are scant, they send their children to the mills under the stern pressure of want. The voice of natural affection is entirely overborne by the hoarse croak of hard necessity consequent upon inequitable distribution in the industrial system which enfolds them.

The selfish and cowardly defence sometimes put forward by those who are willing to make gain by exploiting the immature labor of little children is preposterous. " We could not carry on our business without the little folks. It would cut off our profits. We could not compete successfully with the other mills. We would be compelled to scale down our handsome dividends and to deprive ourselves of some of our wonted luxuries." Is not a luxury which maintains itself by consuming the flesh of boys and girls a grave menace to those who enjoy it—is it not more after the spirit of cannibalism than according to the spirit of Christianity? The very thought of cannibalism direct and physical has become intolerable to the civilized world; and the whole habit of living upon the life-blood of others, poured out though it maybe at a little distance and served up in toothsome factory dividends or in appetizing profits, wrung from enterprises which do not pay a human wage, or which make merchandise of the unripe strength of little children, must likewise become intolerable! In the presence of all such selfish materialism and gross disregard for the present and future interests of others, it is imperative that this old demand for a sacrificial life should be pressed home ceaselessly upon the modern conscience.

In several States of the Union bills were introduced at the last session of their legislatures making illegal the employment of children under twelve in the factories, or the employment of children under fourteen in the factories between the hours of seven P.M. and seven A.M.; yet, in a number of these States certain powerful corporate interests resisted, and resisted successfully, the enactment of such a law. Even this modest standard of decent regard for the tender growths of our common humanity was too high for them—they could not attain unto it! The child-labor bill introduced at the last session of Congress for the regulation of these matters in the District of Columbia sets forth certain requirements which seem altogether reasonable and just. It provides for the prohibition of the gainful employment of children under fourteen years of age, except in agricultural communities, where farm-labor outside of school hours is exempted; for the prohibition of night work between the hours of seven P.M. and seven A.M. for all boys under sixteen and for all girls under eighteen years of age; for the limitation of the hours of work for all children under sixteen to eight hours per day and to forty-four hours per week; for the requirement of an employment certificate for all boys employed between the ages of fourteen and sixteen, and for girls between the ages of fourteen and eighteen, said certificate to certify to the normal physical and educational development of the applicant for employment; for the absolute prohibition of the employment of children under sixteen in any occupation injurious to health or morals—the occupations thus prohibited to be designated officially once each year by the chief public health and public education authorities in the district where the child resides.

The importance of this last requirement is instantly apparent to those who have seen boys of twelve and fourteen serving as messengers for the delivery of telephone messages and telegrams to women in houses of ill repute; or boys of that age employed in the bars and rathskellers of large hotels, where they hear the ribald jest and obscene story and witness scenes which must corrupt and degrade; or boys employed as pages in certain theatres, where night after night they witness " problem plays " or other unseemly performances, and are brought in contact with men and women whose influence is debasing. The wrong done to the messenger boys has been pressing for attention in several of our cities. It was brought out by the testimony of the police officers in the precinct covering the vicious quarter in Washington, D. C., that boys as young as ten and eleven had been seen answering calls to houses of ill repute by day and by night. " These houses have their call-boxes, and any foul creature can, by pressing a button, have a boy of tender years sent to her at once to place himself at her service for any errand of evil which she may wish." And the sad fact is that this service appeals strongly to the boys, both because of the curiosity of those who are in process of discovering the mysteries of sex life and because these women are more generous of their tips, perhaps, than are the people in respectable parts of the city. For any corporation, in order to increase its profits by saving the larger wage which a mature man would require, to thus send young boys into these places is altogether damnable; and it argues great moral callousness that our communities are willing to tolerate, and, in the cheaper service enjoyed through the employment of the immature, to profit indirectly by this detestable practice! That larger habit of mind which looks steadily upon the higher interests involved in any course of action and resolutely subordinates private interest and convenience to the higher good, is as sorely needed to-day as it was when the God of Israel began to educate His people along that line in the prescribed system of sacrifices.

One of the hopeful facts about the labor union is that it does call upon its members to make sacrifices for the common good. You will find abundant illustration of this in almost any wise and just strike. Working-men are commonly loath to strike, so long as it can be avoided without an injustice which seems to them unbearable. In the event of a strike their employers will suffer some loss—they may be cut off from some of their accustomed luxuries, but they will not, in all probability, be reduced to anything like want. The strikers themselves will be out of employment, which in itself is a menace to moral as well as to material well-being. They will be compelled to economize their resources strictly because all income has ceased. They will oftentimes be compelled to watch their wives and children grow ragged and thin. They will see the little store of savings, patiently built up by self-denial, waste away. They may be driven to incur at last the plague of debt, to be a grievous burden for months to come. They may even have to stand by and see other men, single men, perhaps, who can work cheaper than those who have families to support, or negroes from the South, or cheap Asiatic laborers, brought in to take their places. This is what they may be compelled to face if the strike is ordered, and surely, in their willingness to do all that for the sake of a principle, they give evidence of a spirit of sacrifice which subordinates immediate personal advantage to the general good of the class to which they belong.

The recently published book of John Mitchell on "Organized Labor" gives an unimpassioned discussion of the present situation in that part of the world of manual labor with which his personal service has made him familiar. In all the reviews of this book which I have read, many of them unfriendly and written by men who were entirely out of sympathy with labor-union methods, I have not seen a single statement of fact made by Mr. Mitchell called in question. The most interesting pages, perhaps, are those in which he relates, without flourish or rhetoric, the account of the great coal strike of 1902. The coal operators, always insisting strongly upon a duty on coal " to protect American industries," had nevertheless encouraged the immigration of Poles and Hungarians, Austrians and Italians, in order to lower the rate of wages, until one hundred and forty-seven thousand of these anthracite coal miners were here at work. For years these miners from the south of Europe had been unorganized, and had in consequence been suffering from low wages and long hours, from unjust " docking " and exorbitant charges for powder, from the exactions of company stores and from the fact that their average yearly employment was only one hundred and ten days. They were living, many of them, in rude huts and on scanty fare, with few or none of the privileges and advantages of twentieth-century civilization. And because of the narrow yearly income their boys were put upon the breakers or into the mines when they ought to have been in school; and the girls were thrust into mills and factories by the same hard necessities of their families.

It was a difficult task to organize these untrained men, differing as they did in language, in race, and in religion. Many attempts had failed, but finally the one hundred and forty-seven thousand anthracite miners were brought together, and after repeated conferences they agreed upon a method of procedure. When their desires were made known to their employers the operators bluntly refused to arbitrate the matter or even to meet the representatives of the miners. The men were thus repulsed at the very outset, yet for weeks and months they endeavored to avoid the strike from which they knew that the whole country, as well as themselves, would surely suffer. But at last, for lack of any other course of action which promised relief, they went out in one of the greatest strikes of modern times.

During the summer they cultivated their little garden patches; they lived as long as they could upon their scanty savings and upon what they raised by pawning their watches and other possessions. But by and by their slender resources began to be exhausted and actual want was staring them in the face. The bituminous miners of the country then came to the assistance of their fellows and voted to give a tenth of their own wages, and the officers of the unions offered to give a third of their salaries, to keep the anthracite miners alive until they could win out. The British Federation of Miners also sent five thousand dollars across the sea to brother miners, whom they never saw and never expected to see, to aid them in their struggle. These men, who were striking for a human existence, were hungry and needy; they looked out through their narrow windows and saw the wolf at the door, but they stood firm for a principle. There was undoubtedly violence here and there on the part of the strikers, for these one hundred and forty-seven thousand miners were men and not angels, and they were hungry and oppressed men—and for this violence no honest defence can be or ought to be made; but their moral heroism as a class, considered in its entirety, and the stout adherence to principle displayed were splendid!

The strike went on for months, until finally the President of the United States invited the coal operators and John Mitchell to meet him at the White House. The miners, through their representatives, offered at once to submit the whole matter to any board of arbitration selected by the President, and to abide by its decision. The operators refused to have the questions at issue thus arbitrated. This effort of President Roosevelt therefore failed and the strike continued, until at last, through the intervention of a New York capitalist, such pressure was brought to bear upon the operators that they yielded, and the matter was finally submitted to a board of arbitrators selected by the President. The final award of this board of arbitration granted almost every request the miners had made, showing that their main contention was just and right. And, their cause being just, we cannot but feel that their heroism in waiting, their stern and long-continued self-denial, the readiness of their brother workers to give the tenth of their wages to aid them in their struggle, all give evidence of the extent to which the spirit of self-sacrifice and devotion to the general good of their class has come to prevail among the toiling masses. And it is only by some such sympathetic and concerted action upon the part of all the members of society acting together, in the interests of that still larger well-being which shall include in its benefits all classes, that the industrial system of the world can at last be made a genuine expression of the purpose of God for all His children.

We certainly have failed to build the civilization God intends, so long as there are so many people in all our cities who prefer to die rather than to live. Ignorant, immoral, misguided souls they are oftentimes, not knowing what death brings, but preferring whatever it may be to the life they are living here—what a comment on the existing social order! The average number of suicides at present is nine thousand each year in the United States alone— in 1905 there were nine thousand nine hundred and eighty-two suicides in this country. These suicides are not for the most part romantic young fools who kill themselves because some pretty miss in pink ribbons has disappointed them. They are more commonly men with gray hair showing above their ears, out of work and out of money, unable to gain employment because they cannot in middle life meet the sharp pace that is set. They look ahead and, seeing no hope, simply prefer to die.

It is a cowardly act for any one to take his own life; the manly course is to stand at one's post and fight the battle through until relieved by the command of a superior. But I personally feel a great and tender charity for those men who, worn out before their time by hard work and long hours, with bodies weakened by insufficient food and nerves depleted by anxiety, make such moral shipwreck. The spirit of consideration and sacrifice on the part of the strong for the weak would prevent a considerable percentage of these suicides, the number of which has become a moral reproach to our modern American life.

The amount of wages which can be paid in a given industry is an economic question; it cannot be settled by quoting texts in church nor by a show of hands at the labor-union meeting. It must be determined in the light of economic facts and forces.

The number of hours necessary for men to labor in a certain business is an economic question—it cannot be determined altogether by sentiment or preference. The men whose main interest is centred upon the spiritual values at stake in the industrial struggle are well aware of all this; but they contend that, in a moral atmosphere created by conscientious men who build altars and stand before them in that spirit of consideration for their fellows which exalts the general good above private gain, these economic questions can be gradually settled in a way which will not be a reproach to our Christian civilization. In that clear atmosphere the choicest personal advantage will look mean and poor if there is a shadow cast upon it by injustice to a brother man. In a society permeated by such a spirit of equity, it will be impossible to endure the thought of a really hopeless condition for the humblest members of our human family.

The account of the actual approach of those Israelites to their future home is also full of instruction. Their man of vision saw the land afar off, from the higher level of thought and feeling where he stood, as from the top of a high mountain. He saw it long before the eyes of the people were able to discern even the more prominent features of it. His eyes outran his own feet, for faith and hope were far in advance of actual achievement. And it was in the strength and courage induced by that lofty vision that he labored on in the face of difficulty and discouragement which would have daunted a less resolute faith.

In sure anticipation of final victory, he sent ahead twelve resolute men, representing the twelve tribes, to spy out the land and to bring back a report. This venturesome excursion into that untried region was, for these forerunners of a better day, a work of difficulty and danger. And upon their return ten men out of the appointed twelve, because of obstacles which they had seen, were opposed to any further advance—they stood ready to give up the whole undertaking!

What a picture of all our brave attempts at progress! Ten men out of twelve come back from the land of Canaan to Israel's camp in the wilderness, saying: ' It is a good land; it is a land flowing with milk and honey; it is a land of fruit and grain, where one eats bread without scarceness and lacks no good thing. But the cities are walled and very great; the children of Anak, the giants, are there— we were like grasshoppers in their sight. We are not able to go up against these people, for the difficulties are very great.' Only two men out of the twelve—Caleb and Joshua, men of vision and pur-

pose—stood ready to commit themselves to resolute
and hopeful action. " It is an exceedingly good
land," these men said, " and if the Lord delight in
us, He will give us the land." Then, as now, it was
to the saving remnant of idealists that society had
to look for genuine progress—to that saving remnant which walks by faith and not by sight, profoundly conscious that the things which are seen
are temporal, but the things which are unseen are
eternal!

But after wandering forty years in the desert of
uncertainty and preparation, the Israelites could not
permanently encamp across the Jordan, looking over
wistfully and fearfully into the green fields of
Canaan. Leaders were sure to arise and cry, " Let
us go up and possess the land, for we are well able
to overcome it! If the Lord delight in us "—delight in us because of the spirit we show and the
methods we employ—" he will give us the land."
Movements for betterment which begin with visions
such as Moses saw when the bush burned with a
mysterious fire, movements which are directed by
such impulses as those which fired his heart when
the divine voice spoke of the needs of his fellow-
men, movements which have encamped before Mount
Sinai until the leading principles of an abiding
moral order have been engraved upon them as upon

tables of stone, cannot be permanently halted, even though ten men out of twelve are timorous and despairing. The men of insight and courage to-day who are saying to the indifferent and the doubtful, " Let us go up, for we are well able to produce something better than these present social conditions," are made strong by this same assurance—they have on their side the same Great Ally. There stands forever on the side of every better impulse in the human heart, every yearning after a truer life, every stirring of the sense of the obligation to others, this same constant, powerful, effective Ally! High walls of difficulty stand in the way! Giants of selfishness and greed, far outranking the children of Anak, oppose our advance! But when the returns are all in, the fact remains that there is One with us stronger than they! And if God be for us, who can be against us?

This better social order which we are to realize does not lie in some far-away country or across the river Jordan. We shall not gain it by travel, but by the gradual transformation of methods and conditions right at hand. The materials for our land of promise are right here upon the ground. The natural resources of earth are more than sufficient for all legitimate need if they are properly used and the results of our common labor equitably distributed. The labor-saving machinery of modern times has made it possible for the industrious man to produce all that he and his family need in fewer hours than ever before in the world's history. The means of transportation are such that, with artificial and wicked barriers taken away, the interchange of those commodities, which can be most advantageously produced by each community, can be readily accomplished. The assessors tell us that the increase of the total wealth in the United States in the last twenty-five years is such as to make the stories of the Arabian Nights seem dull and slow. It is an exceedingly good land, a land that floweth with milk and honey, a land wherein all the industrious might eat bread without scarceness and not lack any good thing. Yet the distribution of these advantages is so imperfect that the problem of poverty in all our great cities is steadily becoming more serious. More than half the families in this land are not now sitting under their own vines and fig-trees, nor have they any clear prospect of ever doing so. Multitudes of men and women are working beyond their strength for an inadequate return, and the lives they live are not the lives of the children of God! Thus, for all those who love their fellows, there remains much work to be done before we really gain possession of our land of promise.

The economic order itself, under the direction of strong, wise, and good men, must become something more than a mere instrument for producing goods. It must become a divinely appointed agency for making men. The ultimate object of all our efforts is the gaining of human values, the working out of high moral results. When " the abundance of things " becomes the main object of desire, these higher ends are ruthlessly destroyed by the wheels of the machine. It ought not to be true that men turn aside from the ordinary work of the week to learn lessons of brotherhood and humanity in the sanctuary, and then go back to the world of industry to unlearn them in an atmosphere of strenuous selfishness. Somehow, the six-days labor must be done in such a spirit, and under such conditions, and with such results, that it, also, shall be a means of grace.

This noble end will be best attained when employers and employed—men of capital and men of labor—bear steadily in mind that further word attributed to Moses, " The land thou goest in to possess is not as the land of Egypt, from whence ye came out, where thou sowest thy seed and waterest it with thy foot, as a garden of herbs." It was a land unlike the valley of the Nile, where men cultivated the soil mainly by irrigation from the great river, the means of production being there quite under human control. "The land which thou goest in to possess," said their leader, "is a land of hills and of valleys," where such irrigation would be impossible. "It is a land that drinketh water of the rain of heaven," inclining the expectant tillers of the soil to look up as well as down for the sources of prosperity, thus cultivating within them the sense of dependence upon some Higher Power. "It is a land which the Lord thy God careth for, and the eyes of the Lord thy God are always upon it, from the beginning of the year even unto the end of the year." The whole prosperity, material and spiritual, which they should there achieve lay unbrokenly within the care and control of the great God above, making imperative an intelligent and obedient coöperation on the part of those who would enjoy the highest well-being.

In like manner the land we go to possess in that more equitable social order which we seek to establish, also drinketh water of the rain of heaven; it is a land which the Lord our God careth for. The well-being we seek is not a thing solely of earth and entirely under human control. It must gain supplies from above and make headway through its effective coöperation with a Higher Power. Those misguided men who are telling the wage-earners to fling religion to the winds, to disregard for a time those finer spiritual values and to enter upon a flesh-and-blood fight for material advantage, are blind leaders of the blind. All such counsel is disastrous; it is sure to react upon those who are foolish enough to accept it, in the lowering of aspiration and the weakening of high purpose. The well-being they seek must forever gain its ideals and principles, its ethical quality and inner spirit, its nobler impulses and requisite moral energy, from the rain of heaven. It must reap its more abundant harvests by the aid of One who, after men have ploughed and sowed up to the limit of their powers, is alone able to give the desired increase. This new social order must steadily look up as well as out in order to gain for itself those higher qualities of mind and heart necessary for genuine and enduring prosperity. Thus, and only thus, shall the Holy City, the New Jerusalem, the justly organized and joyously realized life of men, descend out of heaven from God and be firmly established upon the earth.

It is along this line that the church of Jesus Christ can render its best service—not by devising economic schemes, or by proposing schedules of wages (for the church is not an economist), but rather by shaming low ideals, by overcoming greed, by opposing that lack of consideration between man and man which lies at the root of the trouble. It can diffuse the spirit of equity which shall be oil upon the machinery of industry; it can aid mightily in producing that atmosphere of humane consideration in which the work of social reconstruction can best be carried forward; it can emphasize the moral values at stake, which right-minded men are bound to consider—and thus make its best contribution toward finding " the way out."

It is because many of the well-meant movements for the betterment of the working-people are deficient just here that I believe they are doomed to failure. The programme of the socialist, for example, proposes an industrial system which calls for the qualities of fidelity, unselfishness, and perseverance in greatly increased quantities, yet he seems to be neglecting in his scheme any adequate provision for producing that larger measure of those qualities. " Give us government ownership and government control of all the resources and machinery of production," the socialists say, " and these men who are now selfish, narrow, and false will be public-spirited, generous, and faithful." But will they? What is to reach the springs of action, renew the heart, purify and ennoble the affections, correct and strengthen the will? Thus far no general, abiding, and reliable sense of brotherhood has been attained which did not root down into the sense of a common Fatherhood in God.

The instability of all social organization, which entirely lacks this bond of religious fellowship, is indicated by Noyes in his history of " American Socialism," where he gives an account of forty-five socialistic experiments growing out of the Robert Owen and Fourier movement, not one of which remains—the average life of each being two years. I once sat in a socialist meeting and heard one of the best-known socialists in America make this statement: " No socialistic experiment thus far, on a religious basis, has ever been a financial failure—many of them have gone to pieces for other reasons, but not through financial failure—and no socialistic experiment on a secular basis has ever been a financial success." I am not in a position to pass upon the accuracy of his statement, but if it is true it simply indicates that the only sense of brotherhood which will stand the wear and tear of every-day life in commercial relations is one which is based on the sense of a common relation to God. The prophet of old was right—our well-being, personal and corporate, is not entirely in our own hands; it is a land which the Lord our God careth for; it must drink water of the rain of heaven and look upward for its supplies of grace and truth, from the beginning of the year even unto the end of the year!

In the forward march toward the land of promise we need that deeper sense of immediate and personal responsibility to Him who is no respecter of persons, touching the social bearing of all our actions. The working-men in a certain union may, by their demands, succeed in raising wages and shortening hours. Their employer, instead of curtailing his luxuries to correspond to a reduced income immediately resolves to reimburse himself out of the public, and so he advances the price of his product. The men whose wages have been advanced are able to pay the higher price, but it works hardship to the poor and to all whose wages were not increased—and thus the advance of wages in that one industry works harm to the community as a whole. Thoughtless young women, who have homes to live in and no board bills to pay, go to work in offices or in stores in order that they may have more pin-money for ribbons, feathers, and matinée tickets. They can afford to work for small wages, and are thus prepared to put themselves into effective competition with men who have families to provide for, or with girls who have their own daily bread to earn. In standing ready to accept the smaller wage they thus aid in reducing the earnings of *bona fide* bread-winners. Thoughtless and selfish parents, for the sake of a slight addition to the family income, thrust their children into employment, when they ought to be at school or at play, and by this course stunt the children's lives and reduce the wages of adults by this unnatural competition, making those wages still more inadequate. In all these ways that unwillingness to consider the social consequences of one's course, which lies at the root of many of the vexed questions in modern industry, is manifest. These are difficulties which can only in slight degree be reached by law or enactment—they must be corrected mainly by a deepening of the sense of personal responsibility to Almighty God for all our actions, by the ennobling and enrichment of the inner life.

This brings me naturally to my last point: the gaining of our land of promise is no mere question of securing or of not securing certain material advantages; it is more than all else a question of human values. When I stand upon the shore of the workaday world and look out, I am appalled at the amount of unnecessary wreckage. Men in middle life, worn out before their time by long hours and hard conditions, are thrust aside, as we have seen, and, with a sullen feeling that they have been discredited as men, are doing the work of the women in the home, while the wife and the children earn bread for the family by working in the factory. Women are taken from the surroundings and pursuits to which God has ordained them, robbed of the sweet pleasures of home, of wifehood and motherhood, by the pressure of an insufficient wage on the husbands and fathers, and are thrust into the mill, thus becoming themselves the means of still further reducing that wage. Immature children are cheated of their rights and mortgaged as to their future by unnatural employment. What an incessant loss of fine material is here suffered in this industrial grind!

The fine material is there, beyond a peradventure, hidden away in the ranks of the common people. Now and then a bit of it stands revealed as a sample of what might be realized under more favorable conditions. Moses was the son of a slave, but he framed laws which are to this day as the echo of God's voice against the walls of our human hearts. David was brought from the sheepfold to be the greatest king that Israel ever had, and the Messianic expectation of his race was that One should come and rule who would be " of the house and lineage of David." Martin Luther, the strongest man of his time, one whose service to the cause of intellectual and religious freedom the world will never forget, was the son of a miner. Cromwell, the child of plebeian parents, rose to be one of the best kings that England ever knew, and left as a priceless heritage to the English-speaking race the conception of civil government as a true commonwealth. Lincoln, the rail-splitter, by his eloquence and statesmanship, by the service he rendered to humanity, won for himself the undying esteem of the nations. The common people show an abundance of splendid material, but much of it is forever lost through unjust and adverse conditions.

That old word of Exodus, quoted in a former chapter, comes to our minds again—" the children of Israel hearkened not unto Moses for anguish of spirit and for cruel bondage." Their hard lot unfitted them for making any real response; it dulled their ears to the appeal of spiritual truth. Held down to the hard, anxious, despairing struggle for the bare means of existence, they were in no condition to answer eagerly to the voice of the Spirit or to grow upward into the likeness and image of God. The social question is always more than a question of dollars and cents, of wages and hours; it is a question of human values.

And in view of what is at stake, there is a loud call for Calebs and Joshuas, for courageous idealists and brave fighters who walk by faith, to stand forth and summon other men of courage to go forward

and possess the land of a better social order. The
giants of greed and the walls of difficulty cannot
be allowed to shut us out or to frighten us away.
In a noble unwillingness to make gain by taking
advantage of another's helplessness; in a splendid
consideration for the moral values latent in every
human life; in a higher resolve to show intelligent
good-will toward all whose lives are bound up with
our own; in constant dependence upon Him who
alone can guide us to victory—we are to move steadily up and out of the wilderness of dreary sand and
bitter waters toward the fertile fields which lie
within our land of promise.

CHAPTER VIII

THE BEST LINES OF APPROACH

WE commonly find three views held as to the relation which the ministers of religion should sustain to these social problems. There are those who say that the church has nothing to do with them directly—its whole business is " to save souls," meaning by that, as a rule, the cultivation of individual piety. There are others who behold in the work of solving these social problems a new and better form of religion which is to entirely supplant the old. These persons cast ordinary religious faith and worship quite out of their synagogue; they give their whole strength to the relief of actual need or to the task of improving the common environment. And there are, in the third place, those who are striving for that truer synthesis wherein lies the real unity of the things of sense and the things of the spirit. They know that " God is Spirit," and that whosoever would approach God directly must do so from the side of his own nature which is also spirit. But they know, too, that the common life, with all its

material interests included, furnishes the only fruitful field for the exercise of those powers which are
brought into play by the coöperation of the finite
spirit with the Infinite Spirit. The spiritual life is
simply the natural life lived in a new way—the
natural life ennobled and transformed by an in-
dwelling divine Presence. These men look upon
the common world itself, therefore, as the subject
of a nobly conceived redemption to be wrought out
by flesh-and-blood men acting in harmony with the
divine will. This third view has been gaining steadily on serious, aspiring minds until now, in great
sections of modern society, " there is no longer any
sharp line of division between sacred and secular,
but only a vaster, keener sense of right and wrong."

It ought to be so, for when Jesus sent His servants
out to sow the good seed of the kingdom, He said
to them, " The field is the world." The place where
religion is to grow is not some holy corner of this
human life of ours, fenced off and walled in from
the rest of the common earth. The tired life of
mankind may now and then enter such quiet places
in order to renew its strength, to wash itself clean
in fresh baptisms of divine help, and to feed upon
those forms of nourishment which come out of the
unseen, but it lives its real life out in the open
where men are buying and selling, employing and

being employed, struggling, sinning, suffering, and dying. The field is the world!

We never plant a sequoia-seed in a flower-pot—we plant it in the bosom of mother earth where it may draw steadily upon unmeasured resources in the unfolding of a life which will reach on through the centuries. And we do not willingly plant the Gospel of the Son of God in any narrow enclosure which leaves outside large fields of human interest; the only area which can furnish adequate material for the full expression of the religious life is this total world of common interests. The world, indeed, where men sometimes pray and trust and adore, but where they also struggle and wrestle together from hard necessity in gaining their livelihoods; where they love and marry and rear families; where they organize States, enact laws, and make history; where they think and write, study and teach, organizing the common quest after knowledge into splendid institutions—this big, powerful, complex thing called " the world," Jesus said, is the field where the good seed of religion is to be put down under the surface and made to grow. This field alone is wide enough to furnish that sufficient harvest which Christ shall come to reap.

And in the same vein that seer, who caught a vision of a new heaven and a new earth where right-

eousness dwelt, cried out in his joy, " The tabernacle
of God is with men and He will dwell with them."
With men! Not with a few cloistered saints alone
or with some lonely, pale-faced ascetics living in the
desert on locusts and wild honey—all such, according
to the word of Christ, are " less than the least in
the kingdom of God." The men referred to in the
vision of the seer are city men—men surrounded
by walls huge and high; live, active, efficient men,
ceaselessly engaged in serving Him, busied ever with
the great common interests of a highly developed
life! These are the men with whom God makes His
home, according to that noble vision.

We may say, then, that the presence of God is
to be found and realized, most of all, in the thick
of human affairs. The interests of busy men are His
interests; and His abiding purpose is to bring their
thoughts and their ways into perfect harmony with
His thoughts and His ways, as He dwells with them
in all this varied life. The teacher of religion will
therefore approach these social problems, not as
something foreign to his essential purpose, but as
necessary elements of that " world " which God so
loved as to give His only begotten Son for its complete redemption.

It goes without saying that the true minister of
religion in approaching these vexed questions will

not do so as a partisan, except in so far as the Ten Commandments, the Golden Rule, and the Sermon on the Mount are partisan in their insistence on a higher righteousness. The minister has not enlisted to fight the battle of the capitalist against the wage-earner, or the battle of the trades-union against any employers' association or citizens' alliance—he is fighting the battles of the Lord, whose purposes are higher and vaster every way. He is fighting against all selfishness and greed, against all injustice and inhumanity. His great concern is to aid in an advance toward the point where the work of earth shall be done " as it is done in heaven," as it is done in that state of life where right principles hold fast and bear rule. In the urging of these great principles, I commend to you the desirability of that non-partisan habit of mind which comes with " the view from above " of the real prophet. And I also commend to you the desirability of that quality of speech which was finely attributed to a certain United States senator who died recently—" the eloquence of accurate and temperate statement in the discussion of mooted questions." It is a form of speech which carries further and does more execution in the actual accomplishment of desirable results than the louder, hotter innuendoes which more readily command head-line space and red ink in the modern newspaper.

In this whole effort at social readjustment it is to be remembered that neither political nor industrial organization can be pushed far ahead, if they can be pushed ahead at all, of the intellectual and moral advance. External changes of condition and organization unaccompanied by inner changes of disposition and social efficiency will avail nothing lasting. The minister, therefore, will be conscious that he is usefully employed in the solution of these problems when he is helping to create the social habit of mind, when he is keeping sensitive the social conscience of those to whom he ministers, and when he is increasing that stock of responsible character which alone is competent to administer the more equitable industrial arrangements which a wise benevolence may propose.

I believe, therefore, the best lines of approach for the Christian pastor lie generally in the following directions: In his whole utterance and activity he can exalt the spiritual above the material values until, in another sense than that intended by the prophet of old, he has helped to "make a man more precious than fine gold" through a much-needed revision of the current quotations. "How much better is a man than a sheep?" Jesus once asked, bringing the human values and the property values before the mind for appraisement. Society has never given an altogether satisfactory reply to this radical question. Fine sheep are sometimes sold for five or six thousand dollars each, while the value set upon the human lives of the lowly often seems to be very far below that figure. But all such mistaken ratings have the forces of earth and sky against them—in the long run the human will be seen in the ascendant. No matter though the sheep, standing for the property interests of the world, has advanced in price, while in certain quarters human life has declined until it seems the cheapest commodity to be found, the man, however he may be circumstanced, still outweighs the whole world of material things, even as he did in the days when Christ came preaching the true standard of values.

The relatively low estimate put upon these spiritual values by many of its earnest and popular advocates is one of the weaknesses of modern socialism. It has, of course, many other limitations which need only to be named to be recognized as serious impediments in the way of introducing any such *régime* as that proposed by radical and thoroughgoing socialists. This movement has in recent years assumed more formidable proportions, drawing into it, along with a great multitude of discontented and unsuccessful people, many active minds and earnest hearts genuinely bent upon the amelioration of the

lot of their unhappy fellows. Indeed, the term
"socialism" has come to be used so loosely that
almost any sort of effort at social readjustment is
liable to be catalogued under that general head, and
almost any man who would undertake to aid in securing a more equitable distribution of the good
things of life is apt to be dubbed, either by the hos-
tile or by the sympathetic, a "socialist." In my use
of the term in these lectures, however, I employ it
only in its more limited and definite sense—a socialist, according to the definitions authoritatively announced and currently accepted by the men of this
economic faith, is one who proposes "government
ownership and government control of all the resources and the machinery of production" as the
only direct and effective means of industrial amelioration. This is socialism, and the rest of us, however large-minded and benevolently inclined we may
possibly be, are not regarded as socialists unless we
are ready to advocate this economic programme.

It is altogether superfluous to say that with many
of the abstract ideals proclaimed by the socialists,
I, along with all other humane people, am in most
hearty sympathy. But I do not follow with them
in their advocacy of the economic programme put
forward as the best method of attaining those ideals.
At the very moment when my heart responds eagerly

to many of the ideals themselves, my sober economic judgment withholds its indorsement of the plan proposed for the realization of them. The poetry of socialism is, to a considerable extent, acceptable to all men whose social sympathies are alive and active, but the prose of socialism remains open to serious question at the hands of discriminating intelligence and age-long experience.

The whole movement, with all its plans and proposals, is altogether too elaborate for me to undertake any detailed discussion of it here within the time allowed, but I can, in a few words, indicate the main lines of my own dissent from the position taken by genuine, root-and-branch socialists. The socialist, as we know him in this country, has thus far shown himself an almost entirely negative factor in the life of the community, " shining mainly as a pungent critic of the existing order " rather than by any well-assured ability in outlining the immediate steps to be taken for the introduction of that better order which would more perfectly secure the well-being of the many.

In some of its forms socialism seems like a belated bit of asceticism. The old asceticism claimed that personal freedom, the intimacy of the sexes, and the desire for gain were all productive of evil—it therefore undertook to destroy, in the lives of accredited saints, all these sources of evil and all the hurtful influences which attached to them, by its vows of celibacy, poverty, and obedience to an order, thus protecting its own devotees under the shelter of the cloister. This new asceticism sees truly that private property is oftentimes productive of greed, of oppression, and of divers social wrongs; it feels unwilling to incur the risk involved in private ownership as we know it to-day; it would therefore undertake virtually to abolish the potent influence of private property by merging individual ownership of all the resources and machinery of production in the state. The strong impulse toward useful activity which springs from the hope of gain, liable as that impulse is to serious abuse, would be quite removed by this plan, and the consequent loss of incentive would be so considerable as to make the proposition seem to many of us like another case of burning the barn to get rid of the rats.

The socialist seems also to impose altogether too heavy a load upon a single institution, the state, disregarding too much the great functions of the family, the school, the church, and the voluntary association of men in industrial effort. The degree to which the function of the state in the administration of certain public utilities may be profitably enlarged is a question for economists and statesmen. It will be settled finally, not by oratory, or by sentiment, or by Scripture texts, but by instructive experience. The state is now only fairly successful in the carrying and distribution of the mails, a comparatively simple matter, for all the men on my street and all the people of the city and of other cities want their mails carried just as I want mine—safely and promptly. But if it were a question of the state undertaking to manufacture profitably and to distribute satisfactorily spring bonnets, for example, to meet the wants of the respective wives of all these men, or of proving itself efficient in providing all the ten thousand things where taste and habit differ so widely, as it would be required to do under a system where " government ownership and government control of all the resources and machinery of production " obtained, it might not find itself so readily adequate to the task. It is this vaster duty which socialists seem so ready to lay upon a state which should own and operate all the resources and machinery of production. The socialist seems entirely too willing to say to the many unprofitable servants who somehow get into office—some of them unprofitable from lack of ability and some from lack of honesty—" You have been unfaithful over the few things you have heretofore controlled; we will make you rulers over everything."

Personally I do not believe that private ownership of the means of production will disappear or
that it ought to disappear. I do not believe that all
competition will cease, or that it could entirely
cease, without a loss of incentive to effort which we
are not ready to incur. I do not believe that superior personal endowment and untiring industry
will cease to command a reward altogether exceptional—I think it is best that they should command
such a reward. The exceptional returns now offered
put a premium upon and effectively stimulate the
production of those useful qualities in the lives of
many who might not show themselves responsive to
any other form of motive. The industrial forces
here suggested have caused many to " offend ";
they have been turned oftentimes by unscrupulous
strength against unprotected weakness in ways full
of harm. But they will not, in my judgment, on
that account be " cut off " so that we may " enter
maimed " into such a life as the socialistic *régime*
might be able to offer. I believe rather that they
will be caught and held within the power of a
mightier and more extended consecration, so that we
may at last enter into life not maimed, but full and
complete, with all our powers retained and devoted
to those higher uses for which they were created.

The people of the United States especially have

shown such an invincible preference for personal freedom, and for the exercise of individual initiative, that they will always be reluctant to fall into any root-and-branch socialistic scheme which would so largely eliminate that dominant characteristic of the national life. The spirit of "scientific socialism" is, indeed, too mechanical to meet with acceptance from the freer and braver spirits of any country. It seems like an attempt to freeze people into a living and organic unity by the clear cold of a certain rigid economic system, held quite apart from the other vital forces which have to do with individual and social progress.

The minister of religion, laying as he does strong emphasis upon the spiritual elements involved in the industrial struggle, feels also the incompleteness of "the economic interpretation of history," of which so much is made by those socialistic writers who preach steadily from the text "the want of money is the root of all evil." They seem to be quite unaware of the fact that neither these words, nor the idea expressed in them, have ever gained standing in the accepted Scripture of thoughtful men. Economic conditions have, as I have tried to indicate in these lectures, entered powerfully into the determination of the quality and the direction of the life of many nations, but when all has been said, the fact still stands that the truly sovereign forces of history have not been material but spiritual. The great deeds have been done, the great songs have been sung, the great pictures have been spread upon canvas, the great productive eras have been brought in, and the great movements have been set on foot, not for pay nor through economic interest, but because of the prevalence of certain spiritual ideals which for the hour had become supreme. Therefore, the renunciation of all alliance with spiritual forces and the uninstructed readiness to stake their all upon forces purely economic on the part of many of the poor, the weak, the unfortunate of society, under this mistaken leadership, is one of the blindest of all blind movements into which unthinking people have been led.

In like manner the true prophet will make plain to those who feel that the push of unregulated self-interest can be safely intrusted with the world's progress the fundamental error of their contention. Buds and brutes may be guided solely by the push of self-interest, crowding out their less fortunate fellows as it may serve their turn, but men possessed of reason and conscience have both the ability and the disposition to help one another—qualities which are to be manifested increasingly under the pressure of an ever-deepening sense of social responsibility.

This quality of neighborliness is not in any sense an economic force—it is spiritual and it is of God. It is a force already powerful, which must be constantly taken into account by those who would forecast the future of society.

The world is so made that the way of inconsiderate and unregulated self-interest is hard, and it is destined to grow harder with the growing sense of social obligation. Those men who, in their selfish exploitation of valuable resources and in their narrow indifference to the wider interests involved, are saying, " The public be damned," will find that the stars in their courses are fighting against them. In the outcome, they can hope for no happier fate than that of Sisera. With the same measure they mete to others it will be measured to them again, for there is a rising tide of public sentiment, as well as a God in Israel, neither of which will permanently tolerate human swinishness. Men who propose to build buildings which will stand up and not fall down must build them, whether they like it or not, with due regard for the law of gravitation. And men who would rear for themselves any stable prosperity must likewise reckon with that law of moral solidarity which is equally universal and insistent.

The minister of Christ will also render useful service by aiding in the growth of an intelligent good-

will thoroughly instructed as to the wide reach of
its standing obligations and capable of being carried
into all the relations of every-day life. It has been
said that all the people in the world could live in
the State of Texas, if they were only friends. This
may be a slight exaggeration as to the possible resources of that one State, but it makes plain the
fact that the main barrier in the way of realizing
universal well-being is not so much paucity of re-
source or scarcity in actual production, as the lack
of right spirit in the work of distribution. Men of
intelligent good-will could operate almost any form
of industrial organization within reason and render
it acceptable to all hands—at least to all right-
minded and industrious hands. And, conversely, it
would be almost impossible to devise any political
or commercial *régime* whatsoever, where the shrewd,
the strong, and the unscrupulous would not be able,
if they chose, wantonly to take advantage of the
dull and the weak. So long as the spirit of any
society is " Each man for himself and the devil take
the hindmost," so long the stronger dogs will get
the best bones and the other dogs will stand by
hungrily licking their chops, waiting their chance
to take what is left. In saying this I am not unmindful of the possible benefit of certain economic
readjustments, but as ministers of religion our more

fundamental concern is with that nobler spirit which will inhabit and control the political body and which alone will be found competent to give shape to a higher type of industrial organization.

We certainly have a serious duty to perform, as ministers of Jesus Christ, so long as there remains such a glaring difference between the social ideals professed in the worship of Sunday, and those ideals actually pursued in the business of Monday. Hear these words from a thoughtful discussion, by one of their number, of the present attitude of the working-men of our country to the Christian churches. " The complaint made by American working-men against the churches is that they have failed to sufficiently influence conduct; they have failed to adequately impress their fundamental principles upon those who give direction to the practical affairs of life in the counting-room, in legislative halls, and on the bench, although these men profess Christianity. Laboring men do not feel that it is better for them to work for a Christian than for one who denies the obligations of Christianity—the outcome of experience has not taught them that such is the case. They do not believe that church membership on the part of their landlord insures just and considerate treatment for his tenants. They do not flock to merchants who acknowledge Christ as their Master, in confidence that they will, merely on that account, receive of them honest goods for a fair price. They do not rejoice when they learn that a railway magnate, in whose employ thousands of their number stand, is regularly attending an orthodox church." The very fact that such a charge can be brought against the churches of the land, and the further fact that over such wide areas of the busy world the charge can be so well sustained by evidence as to the truth of it, lays upon our hearts afresh the obligation of urging the expression of intelligent good-will in every-day life as a fundamental requirement in Christian character.

The capitalist, who regards his right to purchase labor in the cheapest market available, regardless of consequences, as being altogether sacred, and who conducts his business in such a way as to breed discontent and the spirit of rebellion among his employés, is himself furnishing the gunpowder which is liable to blow him and his prosperity into the air. The open disregard for men as men, because they happen to stand in the class of manual toilers, which is displayed in certain quarters of modern industry, has destroyed much of the good-will which is our main reliance for peace and progress. In some sections of our country certain employers of labor, themselves habitual worshippers in the church of Christ are, nevertheless, through the unhalting, unpitying operation of their mills, seven days in the week, sowing the seeds of lawlessness and anarchy by their desecration of that day sacred to the cultivation of moral sanity and of neighborly good-will, as well as to the securing of physical rest and recreation for all the weary toilers of earth. In the face of all this transgression of the law of Christ, it becomes the solemn duty of the minister of Jesus Christ to make plain how much is involved in our praying " Thy kingdom come," and what is the definite content of a pious wish that the divine will may " be done on earth as it is done in heaven."

The minister can also aid mightily in shaping public opinion. In the last analysis our government is a government by public opinion, and the world of business is keenly sensitive to changes and movements in the popular mind. Public opinion under the feudal system was once so negligent of the interests of the serfs as to accord the baron the right to practise such frightful cruelties upon his helpless dependents as would almost stagger our modern belief. We have long since advanced beyond such wanton disregard for the rights of others, but there still remains much land to be possessed by a more resolute public opinion which shall make equally infamous some of the practices of these modern barons. The reluctance of many corporations to adopt all possible precautions against accidents, the unwillingness of many railroads and factories to safeguard the lives of employés with all the appliances which intelligence and experience may provide, until they are driven to it by law, the miserliness shown by certain employers in failing to make any adequate provision for the maintenance of health, modesty, and the finer sensibilities on the part of female employées, must all come in for condemnation at the hands of a more enlightened and more insistent public opinion. This sentiment when fully developed will declare itself in a higher sense of business honor, in more wisely framed and more rigidly enforced laws touching the abuses named, and in a more conscientious giving or withholding of that common esteem which reputable business men are not ready to forego.

This more enlightened and insistent good-will is entirely consistent with material enrichment—indeed, in the long run it is an essential element in a genuine prosperity. Jacob Riis has shown repeatedly from his accumulation of experience at first hand that the love of one's fellows and five-per-cent profit on tenement-house property in New York can live together in peace and harmony. Alas, that man's greed so often puts asunder what God in His wise purpose has joined together! Some years ago George Peabody invested two and a half millions in providing decent tenements for the poorer people of London. It does not seem a large sum with our current standards of expenditure and benevolence, yet twenty thousand people have pleasant and healthful homes at rents which they are able to pay, as a result of that one investment; and the capital has already doubled itself, thus doubling the resources of the trustees who have charge of that effort for the normal housing of the poor. When once this " good-will on earth," which was the main theme of the angels' song at the ushering in of the Christian dispensation, shall overshadow the selfish greed which has too long usurped its place, then the kingdom of heaven will come with power and great glory!

The minister will also insist steadily that there is a will of God in all these matters of common interest, to be discovered, to be obeyed, to be realized, in the organized life of men. When the Israelites entered in and took possession of the land of Canaan, they made a determined attempt to adjust their economic arrangements in accordance with this high ideal in the division of that land. The effort to ascertain the will of God was made according to the customs of the country and the current belief at that early time—they sought to eliminate the element of human greed and of human preference by casting lots. Their leader Joshua assembled the representatives of the tribes at Shiloh before the ark of Jehovah, and there, in the presence of what was to them the earthly residence of their Deity, they prayed and cast lots to determine, according to what they accepted as a revelation of the divine will, the distribution of the land which the Lord their God had given them.

However imperfect, however superstitious or even whimsical the method they used in seeking to know the mind of God in the matter, how much it means that the chosen people in that rude period of the world's history did not undertake to divide up the common wealth by force, the strong taking the best of it because they were strong, leaving the fragments to the weak! How much it means that they did not divide it up solely by the power of purchase, those who had the longest purses taking the choicest sites, leaving to the poor the less desirable tracts! They sincerely tried, as best they knew, to ascertain the divine will in the matter and to divide up the land according to that ascertained will. It was a splendid ideal, however imperfectly they may have worked it out.

God cares about this distribution of goods which

goes on, equitably or inequitably, under His great
eye. God cares about these inequalities of condition among His children, so glaring oftentimes as to
be cruel. God cares that the weak are here and
there thrust aside by the shrewd and the strong, and
thus defeated in the dearest and noblest desires of
their disappointed hearts. There is a will of God
concerning all these questions as to wages and
hours, as to the appropriation of land and of mines,
as to the enjoyment of luxury or the suffering of
penury. And our own commonwealth will never
measure up to its full moral dignity, it will never
attain that full degree of stable prosperity, where
each family shall sit beneath its own vine and fig-
tree, until, in ways appropriate to our day, wise and
good men are equally intent upon knowing the will
of God touching all these interests, and of obeying
that will in the current distribution of the goods
of life.

The great problem of society is not now one of
production but one of distribution. In the hard
times, when thousands of people are hungry and cold
and in rags, there is food enough and fuel enough
and clothing enough to make them all comfortable
—the trouble is they have not the means at hand
to purchase what they need. During the famine in
India, whole ship-loads of wheat were sent from

India, which was starving, to England, which was comparatively well fed—the well-fed people of England had money to buy the wheat, the starving people of India had not. The City of New York is the richest city in the world—you are bewildered when you read of the wealth in its banks; you are amazed when you go to its costly hotels or restaurants and see people being dined and wined in showy extravagance; you are startled when you witness the scale of living at its clubs and in the homes along Fifth Avenue; you are astonished when you look upon the signs of splendid prosperity among the worshippers in its well-to-do churches. It is the richest city on the globe! And yet, in the year 1903, sixty thousand four hundred and forty-three families in New York City, one-fourteenth of the whole population, were evicted for non-payment of rent! Some of them were scamps trying to take an unfair advantage of their landlords, but the great mass of them were people who were simply too poor to pay for a place to lay their heads, and so they suffered the indignity of being put out into the street to await the coming of some charitable agency for their relief. And in the year 1902, according to the "Report of the Department of Corrections," quoted in Robert Hunter's "Poverty," one-tenth of all the people buried from the city of New York were

buried at public expense in the potter's field! You
all know how the poorest of the poor shrink from
such a fate as that for their dear dead, making un-
told struggles and sacrifices to avert it, and the fact
that one-tenth of all who died were thus carted off
to the potter's field gives indication of the great
and sore poverty in that richest city of earth.
Plenty for all, yet the work of distribution so badly
done that this crying want exists even in prosperous times! Surely we have not yet realized the
will of God in our division of this rich land of
promise.

The realization of this divine purpose regarding
our use of the material resources which God has
here placed at the call of energy and intelligence,
will not come solely or mainly by the practice of
a more generous benevolence when once the goods
have been accumulated—it will come rather by the
introduction into the process of accumulation itself,
of a deeper sense of social obligation to all those
whose interests are bound up with our own in that
enterprise, and by the infusion of a finer spirit of
neighborly regard into the mode of ministering to
their life. This point has been clearly stated by
one who has made us all his debtors through his
many wise and just words regarding the social problems now before us. " I do not believe that any

more charitable, any more divine use of money can be thought of than that which is involved in the furnishing of honest and healthful work, and in the manifestation, through the friendships which association in work makes possible, of the true spirit of brotherly love. The man who can gather men about him in some productive industry and can thus enable them by their own labor to earn a decent livelihood, and can fill all his relations with them with the spirit of Christ, making it plain to them that he is studying to befriend them and help them in every possible way, is doing quite as much, I think, to realize God's purpose with respect to property and to bring heaven to earth, as if he were founding an asylum or endowing a tract society." These words are quoted from Dr. Washington Gladden's little book, " Ruling Ideas of the Present Age," and they point out clearly a line of social service which ought to enlist a still larger section of the commercial enterprise, brain power, and moral energy of our American business men. The utilization of special executive ability and the administration of large property interests by some man of means in such a way that the industrial enterprises under his control are, in all the ramifications of their influence, socially helpful and not socially hurtful, thus becomes one of the highest forms of useful service which can be rendered to any community. There are those who do well at the call of Christ to "leave all and follow him," and there are many others, appointed to a different form of service, who also do well to retain their possessions, as did those men in the parables of Christ, to whom both talents and pounds were committed, and to "follow him" by utilizing those possessions with such wisdom and fidelity as to increase the well-being of entire communities.

We are still compelled to walk, as did those ancient Israelites, by faith. Long before they had completely conquered it, they divided up the land, according to what they believed to be the divine will, in anticipation. When the scene which I have described took place, the mountain set off to sturdy Caleb was still held by the sons of Anak; a large part of Simeon's territory was still controlled by the Philistines! As Joshua said, there remained all about them much land to be possessed. But with faith in God that these splendid ideals of theirs could be worked out through His Almighty aid, they met at Shiloh and parcelled out that very soil still so largely under the control of the enemy. "This is Judah's; this is Asher's; this is Simeon's; and this is Benjamin's," they said, even while the Amorites, the Jebusites, and the Hittites were in open possession! The division made was the announcement in faith of certain high ideals which under God's guidance they proposed to realize by the long and patient struggle which followed.

Alas for the dull-eyed, humdrum people whose aspirations never get a rod in advance of their present achievements! Unless we perpetually see visions and dream dreams, we shall never have the moral vigor, the spiritual insight, the noble effectiveness necessary for winning a land of promise. It is what we see by the eye of faith and confidently wait for that kindles our hearts to undertake the higher tasks in life. If we only computed what can already be measured off by the surveyor's chain or weighed upon the hay scales, making no allowance for those hidden and supernatural forces which are ceaselessly at work around us and within us, we should fail utterly. It was one of the evidences that these Israelites were a chosen and inspired people that their plans reached out into a hoped-for but unrealized future, when they divided up great stretches of country still in the hands of their foes.

It is for modern prophets, then, to make it plain that there is a will of God in regard to these alluring social ideals which are being held before men of aspiration, and that the strength of His Almighty arm is pledged to the realization of those ideals when once the hearts of His people are strongly set upon their attainment. It is for these modern prophets to aid in still further developing that spirit of humanity which, awakening from its selfish, riotous life, is saying with a force and meaning hitherto imperfectly appreciated, " In our Father's house there is bread enough and to spare, and yet many perish with preventable hunger." The real problem is one of distribution, and when once the spirit of society shall " come to itself " it will, in the more equitable methods of its operation, hasten the return of multitudes from " the far country " of physical want and moral degradation.

And once more the minister will disclose to his people those deeper sources of motive for social effort. These do not lie, in my opinion, chiefly in the gratitude and esteem of men, or in those glowing promises of reward in the life to come, but rather in an enlarged sense of the abiding worth of human nature itself as authoritatively declared in the great fact of the Incarnation—a truth whose social implications are as yet but dimly recognized; and also in the reënforcement of the sympathetic impulses by vast additions of knowledge regarding the full bearing of our actions, until at last the highest reason and the warmest generosity shall join hands in an invincible alliance.

The strongest motive for personal righteousness, it seems to me, is social in its nature—it is that one named in the great word of Christ uttered in the Garden of Gethsemane: " For their sakes, I sanctify myself." Here He was on the night He was betrayed, walking among the olive-trees, where the shadow of the cross lay upon His pathway. The betrayer had withdrawn from the company of disciples and was yonder plotting against his Master in the dark. And here at last the Lord of the ages knelt in prayer, pouring out mind and heart to One who understood the strange significance of all those events which were crowded into that wonderful week. " Father, the hour is come. I have finished the work thou gavest me to do. I have given them the words thou gavest me. For their sakes, I sanctify myself, that they also may be sanctified through the truth." There was the motive underlying it all —He found the supreme demand for His own righteous, useful, redemptive life in that great fact of human need. For their sakes!

It is a motive which holds where other motives fail. When righteousness no longer seems worth while on grounds of personal prudence, the fact stands that this ignorant, sinful, suffering world needs upright and serviceable men in it more than it needs aught else under heaven. For its sake, then,

I will do my utmost to furnish it one more such life.
It is a motive which offers the strongest deterrent
against the common vices, for no one perishes alone
in his iniquity—of necessity he drags down others
with him from the higher levels of peace and joy
where they might have walked. " For their sakes,"
the sorely tempted man says to himself, " I will live
a clean life! " It is the strongest incitement to useful service, for the consciousness of having made
genuine contribution to the well-being of one's fellows by noble living transcends all those satisfac-
tions which are only personal in their range. " For
their sakes, I consecrate myself "—it uncovers a
source of motive which is like a well of water springing up into everlasting life!

You have noticed in the Lord's Prayer that the
words " I " and " my " and " me " nowhere occur.
The individual considering himself and praying for
himself, all apart from any sympathetic interest in
others, never has a chance to be heard in that ideal
prayer: " *Our* Father." " Give *us* this day *our*
daily bread." " Forgive *us*, lead *us* and deliver *us*."
It is the utterance of a warm, sympathetic, prayer-
ful heart looking out and looking up, strongly possessed with the desire to help. The petitioner casts
in his own need with the rest, seeking to gain his
individual help through the service he renders to

all those whose needs are contemplated in the social terms of this incomparable prayer.

Here we stand, ten of us, we will say, climbing the rugged face of a glacier or some steep snow field, on our way to the top of an Alpine peak. Knowing the danger, the guides have roped us together. We are all members one of another in a most vital sense. It brings a feeling of security. Each man is conscious that he is not left entirely alone to recover himself hastily from the result of some awkward slip—he has nine other men to aid him in that effort. But it also brings a new sense of responsibility. If any man should refuse to put his feet in the niches cut for him by the hands of experience, or if he should in any wise move recklessly, he might fall in such a way as to dislodge the man behind him and they two might drag the whole group over the precipice or start an avalanche which would sweep them all away to sudden death. " For their sakes," each man repeats to himself, " for the security and welfare of the other nine, I will order my course with care and conscience ! "

And we are all thus bound together in families and social groups, in business undertakings and in political life, in educational and church work. It becomes, then, the act of a scoundrel to live in such a way as to imperil the happiness and welfare of the whole group of persons whose interests are firmly roped in with his own. In common decency he must consecrate himself to those higher, wider ideals held before us in this Gospel of the kingdom. If the searching implications of the moral solidarity of men, intensified as it is by the close-knit relations of modern society, can be held before the minds of people steadily and winsomely, until they have become an abiding part of the Christian consciousness, it will add to the vigor of this motive for righteousness, in some cases thirty, in some sixty, and in some a hundred-fold!

This journey toward our complete and permanent well-being is a perpetual journey. We are pilgrims and sojourners, as our fathers were, and our great-grandchildren will be restlessly engaged in the same quest. It is not to bring about immediately some state of existence which will be final and satisfactory that we are wrestling with these problems. It is rather to gain a more social habit of mind and a more equitable rule of life, to level up the pathway of progress and to make the rough places plain, so that all flesh in its perpetual advance may know the salvation of our God.

It is not true now, nor do I see any indications of its ever becoming true, that broad is the gate or easy the way which leadeth unto life, in any of its more worthy forms. There is no sort of encouragement given us that the idle, the shiftless, the unprincipled will ever inherit the earth, no matter what type of industrial system may be in operation. "Strait is the gate and narrow is the way"—the fool, the knave, and the idler cannot enter in thereat. Men and women who are looking for a new heaven and a new earth wherein dwelleth ease and idleness for all hands, an existence untroubled by the necessity for continued exertion, are doomed to disappointment here—and, it may be, hereafter as well, for in a world where the Father has worked hitherto, works now, and is to work henceforth and forever more, it is almost certain that His children will work also. Those who are giving serious attention to social problems are not, therefore, beckoning people forward to quiet and secure ease—they are rather intent upon the permeation of the working-world by a new spirit, making all these employments of hand and brain forever new through a higher type of character placed in control.

The church is naturally conservative as to all projects of hasty reform. It directs its efforts mainly to increasing the amount and enlarging the content of that righteousness, individual and social, which constitutes its major study. It seeks, indeed, to quicken and strengthen human sympathy with want and pain, but it must seek still more to deepen also the sense of equity and justice which shall serve over wide areas to decrease the occasion for such charitable efforts. If it can steadily exalt the spiritual above the material values until that just appraisement shall become an abiding part of the moral consciousness of our race; if it can promote an intelligent and insistent good-will among men as the one informing principle capable of producing a stable, prosperous, and joyous society; if it can impress upon the heart of mankind the fact that there is a will of God in all these industrial matters, which must be ascertained, obeyed, and realized before we can stand right with Him; and if it can discover and lay bare to the faltering will those deeper sources of motive for social effort, then the church will be rendering an incomparable service. This does not involve such a knowledge of economics or of political action as would qualify it for statesmanship, but it does involve a fuller understanding of the real content of the Gospel and a fearlessness in making thorough-going application of its principles to modern conditions.

If in this course of lectures I have seemed to lay disproportionate emphasis on the work of bringing up the rear guard, on aiding the ill-equipped, on making the path smoother for feet which are lame and tired, and have not seemed to give suitable attention to the work of developing and training those who need nothing but an open field, a free fight, and no favor, I would remind you of this abiding truth: The honor and growth of those to whom God has given ten talents cannot be more directly or permanently secured than by the enlistment of that superior ability in the service of others less abundantly endowed. It was said of One whose native endowment so far transcended what is usual, even among men of eminence, as to produce a widespread conviction that He was more than human —" He counted it not a prize to be on an equality with God, but took upon himself the form of a servant, and humbled himself, and became obedient unto death, yea even the death of the cross! Wherefore "—along this very line of self-sacrificing usefulness—" God has highly exalted him and given him a name which is above every name." There is nowhere to be found a more direct road into the supreme development of personality than the road already mapped out in the life of Him who alone was competent to call Himself eternally " The Way."

When you leave these quiet halls you will go out into a troubled world to preach the Gospel of the kingdom. You will go out as divinely commissioned heralds of that nobler order of life ruled by the divine Spirit. When you look up, you will see that peace and harmony are already established in those celestial regions where the heavens declare the glory of God and the morning stars sing together in an endless procession of praise. But when you look out upon the restless life of earth, you see a mass of confusion and disorder which appalls you. The world of material things, where all is passive and obedient to the divine will, is, indeed, a cosmos, but the world of free and intelligent spirits, many of them unresponsive and resistant, is, in great sections of its life, as yet a chaos, waiting for the Spirit to move upon the face of its troubled waters.

You are called, as ministers of Jesus Christ, to be the effective instruments of the divine purpose in the shaping of that highest of all its visible expressions, a society of free men acting together in the spirit of intelligent good-will. If you strive to make your own adequate contribution to the realization of that great ideal, you will find it a task which will steadily tax all your powers to the utmost. It will demand the entire consecration of those abilities which have here been trained for noble service, and it will throw you back unceasingly upon the aid and guidance of Him whose vast design it is to make this redeemed humanity His dwelling-place, and to shape the rightly ordered life of men into a holy city where He shall reign forever and ever.

THE END